SINGER BEWARE

SINGER BEWARE

A Cautionary Story of the Singing Class

Robert Tear

with illustrations by Robert Organ

Hodder & Stoughton

First published in 1995
by Hodder and Stoughton.
A Division of Hodder Headline PLC

10 9 8 7 6 5 4 3 2 1

British Library Cataloguing in Publication Data

Tear, Robert
Singer Beware: Cautionary Story of the Singing Class
I. Title
782.1092

ISBN 0 340 63810 9

Typeset by Hewer Text Composition Services, Edinburgh
Printed and bound in Great Britain by
Mackays of Chatham PLC

Hodder and Stoughton
A Division of Hodder Headline PLC
338 Euston Road
London NW1 3BH

To Hilly, Becky and Lizzie.
Also to two teachers, both dead:
Julian Kimbell (voice) and Alan Watts (soul)

Man's life is a day. What is he, what is he not?
Man is the dream of a shadow. But when the god-given
  brightness comes
A white light is among men, and an age that is kind comes
  to birth.

Pindar, Eighth Pythian Ode

Max at the Audition

With his lute strung from his shoulder, he dismounted from his piebald palfrey and strode to the castle door. The season was that of mists and fruitfulness. As the door was opened to him, sounds of merriment reached his ears. Warm air encircled him and the smell of roast swan was quite delicious. Baron Brassbound welcomed him and invited him first to sup and perhaps, when he was replete, to sing.

'Well, thou merry knave,' said Brassbound. 'What hast thou for me? What wilt thou chirrup in thy sweet way? Will it be the "Vingt-quatre Pucelles d'Inverness" or "Hey diddle-diddle, th'art on the fiddle"?'

'Fiddle, my lord! What a jape, thou know'st I am a mere lutenist with a passing fair voice. But in answer to thy kind question, I have written a new ditty especially for thee, my lord. It is entitled "Nell from the North" and explores the history and quizzical ways of this Esquimaux damsel. But no more talk from me, Baron Brassbound. I'll sing instead.'

And sing he did. The Baron, nay all the court was mightily amused with the wit of the lyrics and the charm of the air.

When he was finished his mighty lordship said, 'I thank thee, Tiny Willie, for thy talent. Take this bag of gold and get thee hence. Viscount Yreggyb Board will appreciate thy gift and will deal with thee fairly. Get thee gone.'

And get thee went he did.

Such was the life of the singer in Merry England. Or was it?

More likely this would have been the scenario. The job at the court is open. I must come up with something new, possibly blue. 'What job?' I hear you enquire.

'Lutenist to the Court, stupid! And before you say "Who are you?" [Well, you've already said it] the answer is that I am Max

Hughescoq, a gifted, handsome, brilliant lutenist-singer and quoits thrower of heady French descent. Satisfied?'

So the job is on offer. The trouble is, every other double-strung gut-plucker will have heard of it as well. Smalljohn, that snivelling Welsh twit, will know and he's wonderful at self-promotion (the worm). Can't sing his way out of a wet brown paper bag, but he's ordinary enough to be liked. He won't embarrass the castle crowd by taxing its intellect. What a joke. No, he's simple – to drooling, a bit like them. Puts them at their ease – if that were possible for such a tight-arsed, scrofulous crew. No, I simply know I'm not for them.

He pauses (for thought).

I know what I'll do. I'll come up with something really sweet and touching – a bit brainless perhaps, but in the circs that'll be no bad thing. I'll give it a memorable refrain and hope that I'll be in good voice.

So Max Hughescoq begins to invent.

'In my helmet now the bees do hum.'

Yes, it's coming, he thinks to himself. Beautiful onomatopaeic touches. He likes the strophes inordinately. And soon the work is complete.

Max arrives for the audition (in the large hall, mind you, this is serious stuff) and is asked to wait in a small stone room. He notices, absent-mindedly, carved devils above him about to vomit all over him – could this be a warning of disappointment? He is nervous and worried.

Soon his apprehension is confirmed. In walk not only ghastly Smalljohn but also Richard de la Tête, newly arrived from France (probably carrying a bottle of Beaujolais, the creep) in all his finery, and with his hideous nasal whine. You wonder how I know of Max's unspoken reactions? The answer is I know him very, very well. Let's say no more – there are some things which should remain behind the arras.

'*En forme*?' Dick enquires.

'Not really,' Max replies. (OK, I'll stop this third person stuff.)

'Not really,' I say, gently keeping the voice in place. 'Got a touch of laryngitis today. Can't get the chords together at the top. You?'

'Superb.'

You would be, you cocky bastard! I dropped this silently on his shoe.

Meanwhile Smalljohn has been invited to start. Through the door I hear his sentimental flauntings and vacuous warblings. Also, and somewhat disconcertingly, murmurs of approval and genteel applause.

'*Monsieur Richard de la Tête, s'il vous plaît,*' came an English voice. The frog left, farting insolently in my direction.

'*Bonjour*, Dick. What have you got for us?'

'Oh, your honneur, zis and zat. I opes you will like?'

The sinuous drone began.

'*L'amour de moi . . .*'

Not that old ordure again, I thought, getting more and more agitated by the second.

On and on it went, all the old faithfuls.

'*Je suis trop jeunesse . . .*'

I say.

'The king went forth to Normandy . . .'

Order of the Brown Nose, for this, I thought.

'Summer is a-coming in . . .'

3

Whimsy trumpeted winsome in an orgy of chic delight. With each new ladle of caramel and each pinch of saccharine, my mood grew blacker . . . My burgeoning reverie of hate was shattered by a cross-gartered loon.

'We're ready, Mr Hughescoq.' He pronounced my name obscenely. As he led me in he affected to drop his papers, bending provocatively to retrieve them.

The scene would have astonished you. There at an oak table, each with an artificial posture, sat a motley group. Ranged about the lord – who sat in the middle – was a pimpled vassal, a poet (some poet this – more a privy-scribbler, I'd say), a jester (as funny as a wet day in Warwick), an ever-aware, brittle archdeacon, a gloriously pretty nun, the cross-gartered loon previously mentioned, and a snivelling Keeper of the Manuscripts (wearing a vest that had it been wrung out would have given a nice bowl of minestrone).

'Max, old thing, what have you got for us?' The lord had spoken.

'Well, your lordship, rather a touching thing, I think.' In fact, this was my masterpiece. Elegant verses praising the wisdom of age, set to music of beguiling bar lengths, twos followed by threes, every movement the possibility of a hemiola (although this sounds as if it needs a trip to the doctor, it is in fact a device whereby the accent is chucked around in triple tempo).

My throat, already dry with hate, was cleared with little hope of relief. The frog would see my fall.

I began.

'In my helmet now the bees do hum . . .' Here I hummed with subtlety –

'And set their hives in the waning sun.

'Oh to be so when day is done.

'And see no more the barrel of the gun.'

I was about to start the second stanza when the pinch-nosed cleric reedily spoke.

'Mr Hughescoq, it's hardly original, is it, this helmet-bees-and-gun stuff? I do think Peele and Knevel used similar metaphors.'

That's blown it, I thought, rather wishing the barrel of the gun was in my sweaty paws. That's buggered me up for this one.

'Sorry, Archdeacon,' I said. 'I don't have the benefit of your education.'

'Surely you can read? It's all in the court library, isn't it, Amgems?'

The librarian-keeper agreed, blinking his eyes in a toady way.

Well, of course it was all over. The dick-head with the frog's voice got the job. I started again, frequenting the music gossip bars. A position was coming up in Denmark, there was a possibility in Reggio Emilia, another in Clermont Ferrand. I knew all the time that I'd have to travel. It always was the same. They know me too well here. They find me boring. They like being bored – but not by me. I have to chase the money. It won't chase me.

Introduction

The dramatic scene I have just recounted is one enacted daily in our opera houses and concert halls. It remains a constant in the Life of the Singer. The audition, the competition, the fears, the triumphs, the failures – all so sudden – the singer must live with and learn to master. They must not master him. I assume that the conditions – the psychological ones – under which singers work has always been much the same. The nature of the employment prevents its drastic alteration.

Singing is a profession which one can hardly call essential. It rests on the margins of frippery, chicness and downright uselessness. I am not discussing the need for self-expression, which is clearly an archetypical necessity. What I am talking about is the pragmatic nature of our trade – that is, the need of others to employ us. They need us to achieve what they are not able to achieve in themselves, namely to find an expression, mental and physical, which is denied them for lack of a certain gift. As I take vicarious joy when watching rugby, so others find a similar joy in employing or watching singers. Since there are more singers than opportunities, competition will always be strong. This doesn't change.

The nature of singers, too, doesn't change. I believe that those characters tweeting in the previous scenes have almost identical characteristics with those of today. The general nature consists of arrogance, innocence, extreme vulnerability, generosity, obsession, vision, physical awareness, a good instrument. Shake all these up, throw them in the air and a singer will assemble itself on the way down.

These waffles on the immutability of the singing type, the insistence that all is as it was and always will be, cover the fact that I have no intention of writing a history of the singing class. I can see that short histories of the great singers might be of immense interest, also that the relationships between the rich and his emblem, the singer, might be of some worth. It would indeed be fascinating to trace the relationship between the dukes with the Minnesänger and the kings with the Meistersänger. It would greatly amuse me to talk vocal technique with Walther von der Vogelweide, watching his wary one eye the while. But such is not the purpose of this tract, and, as I think I should justify the fact that I'm not going to write some historic document, I feel I must equip myself with some intellectual muscle. Here it is.

'The past is a greasy piglet,' Flo Bear said, while staying for a time at Barnes; her friend Virginia Woolf, concerning the past: 'It is like a fish changing a light bulb' (Rouen, 1912). With such intellectual approval I feel I need not overburden you with a sketchy and perhaps irrelevant tour of the old memory or new library.

Another Audition

Singing at 10.15. Must be up by 6.30 for the body to work properly. Didn't sleep very well with imaginings of many forgettings. One particular dream was horrifying. I arrived at the Felsenreitschule in Salzburg with no idea of what I'm to sing.

The stage manager says, 'It's Ottavio for you tonight. Surely they told you?'

My mind goes quite numb, my body wet, clammy, unhealthy. It is twenty years since I sang it last. I now know only the arias, and those not too well.

'Have you got a score?' I stammer.

'Yes. I'll give it to you after the costume fitting.'

'No, I must have it now, do you hear me, *must*! On the way to the fitting room through the great celestial passages at the top of the building we stop and I claim my score. Still hurrying, I notice it's printed in German.

'Didn't they tell you that we sing it *auf Deutsch*?'

'I can't, I can't! It has to be in Italian.'

'Don't worry now. Let's get on to the fitting.'

'I don't need clothes. I must learn something, anything! How long do I have?'

'An hour.'

'An hour – only an hour!' I was beginning to lose control. 'I'll never do it.'

The clothes are fitted around me as I stand with the book on a stand and try to absorb the notes and strange German underlay.

'Make-up, please!'

Half an hour to go, nothing learned, but I'm looking more and more the part. I'm sweating and whining piteously. Nothing, but nothing, has gone in. I return 'ready' to my room and begin to cry. The overture of doom begins.

'*Herr Hughescoq, bitte.*'

I awake relieved and destroyed.

So, not much of a night. 'Il mio tesoro' was one of the arias I was going to sing at the audition. I was singing for a tranche of the Goldschwanz award. I needed more tuition, but had less money. The Goldschwanz was an ideal opportunity to refill my coffers.

I was twenty-five and had begun to ask myself the rather embarrassing question of how much longer I could hide in the world of study. How long could I linger in the world of not knowing whether I was good, not good enough or plain useless? The prize might stave off that evil day of truth for a term or two. How much 'bottle' did I really have? I was fast realising that courage was of huge importance, and was unconvinced of my ability in this area. My name was down as a candidate. I would go.

The trip from Ealing to South Kensington was slower than usual, with more of the public coughing and spitting at me than would have seemed possible. I noticed a girl on my left reading a shopping and bonking novel. I looked over her shoulder – she was engrossed in the bonking bit on page 69. I wondered how she would get through the day. Handily, I suspected.

At the other end of my carriage I saw a singer I knew. He was dressed immaculately in double-breasted grey suit and sober tie. I considered my own attire. I wore an open-necked shirt, jeans, loafers. Who had it right? I wondered, realising – luckily – that we were both being true to our temperaments and so were both fine. But what would the jury think? I knew that one – at least – wouldn't mind the way I looked. He was a middle-aged tenor of liberal, if not eccentric, views. One was an ageing soubrette (could charm her, with luck) and the other a highly established musical great.

The train stalled at Earl's Court. The girl was rereading page 69. It simply would not do for me to be late. Small dews of sweat began to appear under my pectorals. The driver made an announcement only the gist of which I could understand. There had evidently been an 'incident at Tower Hill'. I thought to myself: Some selfish bugger has decided to top himself and is going to ruin my career. As we waited, my panic took on an ominous calm. I thought, quite suddenly, that this strange in-between feeling was how creation must have felt before the Big Bang, a nothing pregnant with all, inactivated activity, life in death, the consciousness of the unconscious. I was shocked from my reflections as the train began to judder forward. Nothing more of interest occurred. I was too obsessed with my possible lateness to notice much anyway, apart of course from the observation that the girl's cheeks were now much redder than when we started. I met the other singer on the platform and we walked to the conservatoire with devil-may-care feet and a great deal of throat-clearing.

'Pianist anywhere?'

Yes, there he is. He's looking more nervous than me. He's washing his hands under running hot water. My competition/friend has gone somewhere to warm up. I peer through a crack in the door.

There they are. The three wise monkeys sitting at their table. See no good, think no good, and most certainly hear no good.

I've prepared three songs – 'Il mio tesoro', 'Ombra mai fú' and 'Love went a-riding'. I've heard that if they only listen to one, you've had it. I'm as ready as I'm ever likely to be.

'Mr Hughescoq, please.' An icy voice with a mock-deferential tone announced my name, scrupulously avoiding the last Q. Of course I was aware that my name was 'difficult' and I thought perhaps that I should change it. I rather fancied the name Dick van Dyke, but was reminded that it was already rather famous.

'Good morning, Mr Huw Cough.' The icy voice, now slightly melting, still shafted through my perilously brittle confidence. He confirmed: 'We won't want to hear all three songs, just two. You choose.' I replied haltingly, huskily, that I would begin with 'Ombra mai fú'. The beginning of this song looks easy, but the crescendo on the first note is deceptive. I began almost inaudibly and increased the voice, trembling, unsteady as an amateur trapeze man over Niagara. Immediately I thought I should have sung 'Il mio tesoro', but then remembered the coloratura and was not so sure.

At this moment, and with much thanks, my interest was taken by the antics of the judges. The soubrette and the singer seemed to have interests in common. They whispered, they passed glances and notes. Probably arranging a 'bumzen' session, I thought. (Singers try to speak in foreign languages, however dated.) The man on the right was a model examiner, with a kind, old face. I assumed that his age had helped him to his arrangement with goodness.

Then they suddenly became bored. They said, 'That's enough, thank you,' and asked me to talk to them.

The walk seemed a long way – they had only heard one song. I had failed but I had finished. They seemed so cold, such strangers.

'Please sit down, I'd like to introduce etc. etc.,' said the kind voice and face. I sat and waited for the questions.

'If you were given an award, how would you use it?'

I'd rehearsed this one.

'Well,' I said, speaking as a tenor should (high, bright) and looking the soubrette straight in the eyes and then fixing the singer with a macho you-know-how-it-is-mate look. 'I would love to continue my study in Italy, learn the language, take a masters in physical education of the leg-over variety.' I said this last bit inaudibly. 'I would continue my study in France and take a doctorate (in the jambe-à-travers, inaudibly). Of course, I'd stay at home, buy a small motor . . . (inaudible).'

'Thank you, very much, goodbye.'

And thank *you* and goodbye, I thought as I left the room. What a load of past-it-nurks, beetled my next thought. Not sure I could manage her if she whimpered.

What a rich old pageant this life is.

Two days later I opened a letter. They'd given me £10,000.

The Auditioner

As justice relies on injustice for its being and as cold relies on hot to prove its frigidity, as good shines the more through evil and perfection requires imperfection to prove its real truth, so the auditionee needs the auditioner to confirm his necessary usefulness. I speak only in comic philosophic terms, for clearly all these opposites are part of the indivisible whole. I'll now show the preceding scene from the auditioners' point of view. From now I will be the singer on the panel.

Remember the one to the left of the soubrette and to the right of the sacrificial lamb.

Oh, God, could do without going there, I thought as I fecklessly thumbed through my hundred ties trying to decide which one to wear or even if to wear. I decided in the affirmative and chose a rather 'jazzy' number to prove to my fellow auditioners and the young hopefuls that I was no fogey, in fact might be seen as a bit of a liberal, radical thinker.

I arrived at the conservatoire twenty minutes early. I'm a compulsively early type (which shows, I'm told, a natural sense of inferiority). The first object that assaulted my eyes (that is, apart from an immensely unhelpful doorman/janitor) was a piece of mutton with long black hair tottering on spring lamb legs with skin of a brown tanning recently acquired in southern climes.

At 9.30 a.m. I'm ill prepared for brittle 'Dahling, how are you? Have you heard . . . ?' singers' talk. Singers' talk can be bowel-wateringly boring; it is covered with an irritating membrane of respectability, like 'I never discuss my colleagues, but nevertheless have you heard . . . ?' The chat fundamentally, I suppose, is rather like all other tittle-tattle. Who's having whom, how thick some singers are, how stupid conductors seem to be and how mad and impossible directors are. Singers tend to recite their memorised

13

diaries at the push of a button, little realising that few care two-hoots for anyone else's career or successes. I suffered ten minutes of tired chat with eyes that stubbornly refused to sparkle. We walked to the concert hall, met the rather fearsome organiser in blonde bubble wig and the third of the panel. I won't bore you with each soul we heard. I will say something more general. But first a jolly jest.

A baritone comes home unexpectedly and finds his wife in bed with a tenor. He feebly says to the tenor, 'What the hell are you doing?' The tenor replies, 'Oh, Alfredo at the Met, Rudolph in Vienna, Hoffman at the Garden.' Do I hear sounds of riotous mirth? See handkerchiefs stuffed into waiting gobs? See swimmers in the tears of overflowing eyes?

The young candidates are intelligent, charming, sweet and fresh. Each carries equal hope, fear in the brightest of eyes, no dull life-sodden whites to be seen, rather pupils, irises all shine and outline.

The clothes are clean, over-ordered, always old-fashioned, perfect reflections of their teachers' tastes. Those same middle-aged with the life-sodden whites tend to live and dress in an emotional fifties' style. The clothes, the thoughts, buttoned up as if afraid of the possible chaos within, or the fear of failure and death lurking without. (You will notice that most women singers wear dresses for the street that would look better on stage, as if their personalities have been so influenced that they can have no taste outside the over-stated stage design. On the other hand, perhaps they are simply outsized characters with enormous egos). The bright youths with feathers new and sparkling souls listen to them, dote on them and become dowdy. They must be freed.

Each arrives carrying a talent hidden in a velvet bag. The precious item is covered with care. Yet as I look at them I see at each corner and every day an unravelling, a small unpicking – not noticeable to them – but capable at the slightest hint of rejection of speeding up the sides and across the bottom till the talent falls to the floor and smashes in smithereens. Like a piece of porcelain it can be stuck together again, the cracks unseeable ghosts, but the piece, the talent, never the same.

It can be argued that it should not be the same, that the nature of time and life is to develop and alter. While temperamentally I agree with this feeling, believing for example that the cleaning and restoration of art, music and buildings merely masks our own mortality, that in the making new of the old we too are reconstructed, this is the human dilemma, the mortepause, the thing that we thought could never occur because our species was so exalted. Thus we buy ideas of rehabilitation as metaphors of ourselves and in them hope that, if indeed we must die, then at least our creations will not.

My feelings for the young singer will not allow such truth. With a pristine, innocent young ingénue it is a different matter. Being a judge condemns me to being an iconoclast, a philistine. There is no place for sentiment – I might even say love – in this competition. There is no place for either in the hard singing world. It is a brittle world and always will be.

So they appear, each vulnerable, quite damageable. I see, I hear, I feel. How is it possible to divorce an immediate feeling of empathy with a good but faulted performer from the antipathetic to the singer with the perfect roulades of a cold machine. This is the eternal problem. So we need three listeners, each with his own foibles, loves, dislikes.

There are certain singers who, with their first sound, you know are the possessors of that indefinable quality which we nevertheless call with great precision 'something'. These gifted ones show a quality of intangible 'carelessness'. They are absorbed in themselves and yet have absorbed themselves. They seem to be free of temporary fears. They are unaware of the surroundings, and of us, yet they manage by sheer belief in the moment to transform a utility-built hall into a cathedral, or indeed a nightclub, at the brightening of an eye or the covering of a lid. It is a magical talent. I use the adjective with care. It is not for nothing that shamans, priests and magi are poets, singers and painters. I have been brought to tears by such gifts.

Sadly, there are the others not so copiously bedecked. At a different level, in Wales, a dear young candidate comes in, flecky nervous. She is dressed with immaculate care, her make-up speaking hours of delicate industry. She announces that she will sing 'O mio babbino caro'. The ensuing performance was one that will remain with me for some time. Zanily out of tune with a tin roof top, the incompetence unnerved me. I felt desperately sorry. Later I heard that she is partially deaf. The simple soul who gave her pain by encouraging her should be strung off – or is it struck up? I can't remember.

Aschenbach

All singers must interpret their material. Each song is a product of the composer's and poet's imagination. This is a fusion which helps one, usually the music, and denigrates the other. Consider the wonderful verses of Müller, long since eclipsed by the genius of Schubert. Romantic taste could not bear a blending of equals. One must be degraded in the elevation of the other. This is not the place to discuss either poetic virtues or artistic equalities. But Müller is a genius.

All singers must become masters, intellectual and vocal, of their literature. Each must see, and assess, for and within his own capability and expertise. If this is done with individual honesty, a new interpretation of a work will always appear. If it is done in the shadow of earlier greatness and deference, third-rate interpretations will follow. Each man is a new man and must see himself as such.

These being the conditions, I will at various stages of this homily introduce my seeing, my versions of works especially important to me. I will begin with an interpretation of the role of Gustav von Aschenbach in Britten's *Death in Venice*.

Gustav of the Stream of Ashes – what a metaphor! We must ask what such ashes were. At the time I sang this role I wrote a longish critique of the part from both a physical and an interpretative view. I have sung it many times since and have only added an idea or two to my original considerations.

What does one make of the monster Gustav von Aschenbach? I am considering here not the playing of the man, the singing of the man, but rather the psychological make-up of the character – that which informs the acting.

A huge devil begins to appear soon after the first thought. Here we have a man who has been lionised in his country and is regarded as a literary colossus in the outside world. He has an intellect, perfect, huge. Since he has some time in his youth felt insecure he uses the intellectual gift as a wall, indeed as a barbican, behind which his sensitive soul may hide. Gradually, imperceptibly even, the shy soul seems to be forgotten as the power of the golden intellect becomes progressively predominant. It leads him to remark that a certain company (on a boat as it happens) is interminably stupid. It is stupid, it later transpires, because the passengers have not recognised him. In this remark we may note trouble for the man – trouble that bubbles fathoms deep.

The early insecurity will not be forgotten but will continue to knock – oh, so gently and so quietly – at his false, constructed self. The man is now two men, the one unacceptable to himself, the other a required edifice. Such confusion in the soul leads to unexpected panic attacks at unsuspected times. These occur when the man is alone, when the built self is at its most vulnerable. He is thus ready for a mental breakdown.

He has ignored one of the basic precepts of Jung: for a man to be whole and at rest, he must at once accept the dark side of his soul, take gladly to him that which is unacceptable and welcome it into himself.

Aschenbach sees Tadzio and is immediately attracted to him. This is quite unacceptable to his constructed self; his intellect, being the clever jailor it is, immediately turns cartwheels in order that the disturbing feelings can be categorised, ordered and thus rendered impotent. Since he is classically trained and since he has impressed his contemporaries with such knowledge, he quickly delves into these airy yet dubious reaches and surfaces with a concept called 'Beauty' which he hopes and believes will stifle his feelings. The word does have its somatic effect, and for a while he feels calmer.

It doesn't last. The boy smiles at him: the foundations of his construction are undermined and fall in a second. The realisation of the truth, no more girt about with intellectual ideas and lies, strikes his lies, he falls and, as Cocteau says of Oedipus, he falls headlong.

Aschenbach is now in the valley of the shadow of death, occupying his dark night of the soul. His false self, all that which made him a lion amongst men, is gone. Will he – as countless others have experienced – become a quieter man, a man who can now be at one with his own instant, a man who might acknowledge the objectivity of truth, a man who might find redemption? The answer, I believe, is yes. G. v. A. does achieve knowledge; that it was to last for such a short time – his death following almost instantly – is simply one of those ironies which constantly occur. However, as one second can be infinity, infinity is better than nothing.

This journey of the soul must be clearly defined in the playing and singing of Aschenbach. It is quite useless to begin at a point when the man has some sort of knowledge. He must begin an ego, a man of undentable self-esteem. He must effortlessly keep his cynical, ironic position. The great world of the unwashed does not even amuse him, he hardly sees it. He has eyes only for his own movements, he has ears only for his own body. He is too insensitive to notice the other characters – his alter ego – that arrive on the scene. He is also too fearful even to cast a glance on the world. All is a threat, a challenge which might destroy; how prophetic this is. On the boat to Venice he dismisses the passengers and tries to ignore the fop Casanova; at the hotel he deals with the manager like a piece of useless baggage. However, in all this denial he cannot deny the sea. It is for him a symbol – notice that it is a symbol, not reality (that would be too crude) – of freedom in death. He is defeated by the sea at every turn, at every glance. It rocks him, seduces him, it is the glamorous siren sister of the void. In the first Act (apart from his last line, of course) this is the only weakness that he must show.

However, his strange unannounced collapses keep happening, usually when he is in his gondola. They attack, bringing not only physical pain but mental derangement. When he is assaulted by those trying to 'show him places to delight him', his madness devours him. The foundations are cracking. The final breakdown, I believe, must be played with sheer physical revulsion, with the body in a state of shock. This is the moment when the audience, if you are working well, will also be in a similar state. They should leave for the interval as if a sword has pierced them.

The second Act must be played open and destroyed. Nothing now can be hidden. Aschenbach is for the first time in his life in the open. He is a cringeing man, looking through keyholes, hiding behind pillars and newspapers, always getting near enough to touch but never touching. The chase must be played in this abject but totally exciting way (after all, the man has suddenly become young). The energy of passion is on him. The constipating concept has been freed. He is full of self-disgusted joy. Here is his Truth. Joy occurs just when and where it will. This must not be forgotten when playing Aschenbach. Those who spit in the face of joy will never see another day.

The next crucial change occurs in his sleep and dreams. In this state his best and worst fears join in his need for the boy. He says, 'I can fall no further', but he means, 'I am free.'

The Phaedrus dialogue is a posture of freedom and sadness that it carries with it. All that which has perplexed him is now irrelevant. 'Does beauty lead to wisdom, Phaedrus?'

'Yes, but through the senses.'

He could understand the words – or so he thought – but he could not feel. He insists on beauty, but now realises its bodily nature. Phaedrus also says that beauty leads to the abyss, the dark night of the soul or the valley of death.

The singer playing Aschenbach must have passed through this abyss or the task will be beyond him. This leap into the dark is the destruction not only of accepted morality, but also of hope.

Once hope is departed, everything is possible. Desire and hope are gone, the soul is now free. In this abyss is the final freedom of the soul. Here God ceases to care for us – but not we for Him – here, as our desires spit on us, we may soar on mighty pinions. We have become part of that momentous world which is not restrained by our humanity.

When Aschenbach returns – after his one moment off-stage – he is not in control of himself. The self has been sloughed off like the skin of a snake. He is told by the hotel manager that the things that have pleased the *signore* cannot last for ever. This is superficial information. He still believes (a penumbra of his old self believes) that Tadzio will win the fight. The outcome (Jaschiu's victory) is a disappointment, not a tragedy. G. v. A. dies free.

I wish to say very little about Benjamin Britten – at least, not yet – having been too close to him when I had little wit and less wisdom. I would, however, mention that I consider *Death in Venice* a masterpiece. A slightly uncomfortable thought does occur, nevertheless. When I look back and see the last or nearly last works of the great composers, I am struck by the difference between them and Britten. Haydn sums up his thought and belief and produces *The Seasons*, a piece of unadulterated joy and love; Verdi writes *Falstaff*, a work that understands and takes great pleasure in man; Mozart composes his *Magic Flute*, again a piece of unity, imagination and love; Michael Tippett covers the spectrum of mankind and the spirit in his *Mask of Time; The Cunning Little Vixen*, a work of perceived unity of all nature in love, is Janacek's last word. On these great precedents, to find Britten still engaged in a public announcement of sexual preference, and guilt in that preference, I find disturbing. However, this is my problem.

The Performer

An important corollary of being a singer is that as you are confirmed in your sense of worth, so it is taken away. While you attain a certain fame (irrelevant in the eye of death) or notoriety (equally so), you are equally relieved of relevance in the world of political decision. ('A good thing,' I hear people say, and I'm sure they're correct.) Nevertheless, it seems that as you grow as a singer you are relieved of grey matter by a certain internal suction. Although this is of course not true, it is the way in which the singer is seen. He is regarded as a walking gift – a voice unique, floating free, carted round inside a head that has been provided for it and it only. You will find yourself removed, ever so surreptitiously, from those echelons of power that consider and evaluate trends, needs and ideas. You are shunted off into the 'interesting' sidings. You are tied, boxed, into the status of performer.

'Roll up, roll up. Come and see this interesting tigroid, it can sing Electra and Salome . . . And here, my friends, a sweet liger that coos Semele and sparks the Queen of the Night to action. Here to your left a whether, quite excellent for *Messiah*s and lastly in this newly bright and worthy compound, an elegaff simply perfect for Purcell's bass parts.

So we are viewed as quite interesting performing things, the outside, visible nature, all that matters in the world of commodities. It is true that many singers have encouraged this attitude to others by being totally enamoured of themselves and their careers. However, most are not like this. They have a gift, and this they know; and they are mostly highly intelligent and very vulnerable. There is within them a knowledge of an inner emptiness which they know cannot be satisfied with singing. There is no room, in the technical and demanding world of performance, for thinking. No time for inward discussion, little place for the real questions of death, the pursuit of goodness and the metaphysical, or indeed the moral quest. Such time must be found. Inner strength must fill the vacuum which the rind of the singing career creates.

Those who find singing to be the ultimate answer to the question of 'Why?' I find a couple of slices short of a loaf. They are not only immoderately pleased with themselves, but believe, genuinely believe, that others are interested in their progress. They discuss technique with a passion. They will eagerly listen to gossip but will never talk of a 'colleague' themselves. (This word 'colleague' presumes a noble friendship based on the articles of work. The colleague can, however, be the most bitter of rivals.)

Having made such comments about the two sorts of singers, I'm forced quite unwillingly to a conclusion (a simple one). Unwillingly, because it leaves those with total commitment in the right and a dabbler like me on the sidelines.

My argument is that all action needs total concentration. I am not speaking of the instant of awareness that *should* be possible every instant – rather of the need to be obsessed with one thing. This thought came to me when discussing with a friend the romantic theory that great creators had perforce to be good men. Schubert and Beethoven couldn't have contracted syphilis, because that would have removed them from their Apollonian plinths. They had therefore cursed genetically. Wagner had to be a moral giant, because he was an intellectual one. Even today we find the desire to canonise Britten. As these desires clearly fly in the face of the evidence, I was forced to consider why it is not possible for great creators to be saintly. The answer, it seems to me, is that any job done properly needs total concentration. Therefore to be a great composer takes all of the composer, as to be a saint takes a lifetime in the technique of perfection. One obsession will not permit another. They speak of the 'ought' of professionalism. Under this stringent argument my shadow-talking way with music and philosophy and mysticism appears quite vapid. This, however, is the way I am. Perhaps it is my talent always to understand but never to approach too near. Perhaps this – and I now speak in my defence – also gives me a dimension of eternity that forbids my complete absorption in things of changeable brevity and vaulting ego. Who knows anything? The temperament is all.

All this chat, you will have realised, is by the by, and of such a personal content as to render it less than useful to the subject in hand. And yet (have you noticed there's always an 'and yet?'), the nature of existence is that it will be always the same and always quite different. This apparent dichotomy arises in the desire for the self to be different. So, as a singer I am both the same as other singers but also quite unique, and as such I feel I may speak from my individual position in a generalised way; and so with this ditsy introspection I feel I can assent that the singer is always a commodity and that it is always others who decide where he belongs, which role he will occupy, which not. These 'others' who decide such matters of moment are 'dilettantes' – who have made the 'opera' their lives. In this solipsistic world, they cannot be criticised in their belief but they can be in their shallow visions – at least I feel it is so. The fact that others decide your gift always rankles. We know what we can do, what we can't. We understand our distance, our immediacy. Yet others – always amateurs to our eyes – determine, rule, control. Learn this, ye young 'uns. It's a fact.

Old Glyndebourne

I have always been lucky. When this fortune coincides perfectly with what I consider the 'right time', then life and those things that go on within it can indeed appear golden. Of course something will always bring me to my senses; this time a shortness of breath is the dust on the gold, but at least shallow breath is not the harbinger of a cold.

However, this feeling of the rightness of time is on me. The place is Glyndebourne, the part Gustav v.A., my age fifty-three. The alignment is perfect, quite unlike the record of my past career. This time I've not peaked too soon, as their sayings go. This is my debut at Glyndebourne. When I was of the Glyndebourne debut age in the 1960s I was at Aldeburgh singing for the Brittens, and as the Brittens and the Christies had recently warred those who sang in Suffolk tended not to sing in Sussex. For thirty-two years this friendly and lovely place has been kept from me. Nevertheless, everything is now exact for my debut. The production of Steven Lawless is clear and filled with a mysterious Expressionism, the cast perfect and the critical reviews ecstatic. (There is one critic who seems to wish to perpetuate the lie that Mann and Britten used to expiate their guilt. Do you remember the one? Plato used it when he said, 'A man overcomes sensuality when his reason makes him realise that beauty – note the word – is all the more perfect the more it is removed from corruptible matter. What a gift of an excuse for rampant paedophiles or lustophiles. I can understand exactly what Plato is saying, but as a proto-Christian he is guilty of dividing a man into equal halves of body and mind. It is clear that one cannot be without the other. If this fact is not admitted, then lunacy and misery cannot be far ahead.)

So, all considered, an area of loud contentment. I will, during this performance of *Death in Venice* (13 July 1992) try to convey what the condition of this singer is.

I must begin with the general atmosphere. There is a perceptible aura around the place. Just as I felt Aldeburgh to be full of uneasy vibrations and hidden malice, so this place is good. The country, the position of the house lost in the folds of the hills, the easy coolness of landed folk – these are all crucial to this feeling of unforced benevolence. I have never worked with a chorus filled with such evident goodness. (Each member is young, full of hope, each as yet uncorrupted by cynicism.) Some are marvellously wicked, needle-sharp, but I see no signs of maliciousness. Now this could all lie in the shortness of my sight as I teeter on the cusp of senility, but I think not. (I certainly do choose to see *love*, however.)

The oddest thing to a newcomer like me is that, as I quickly realise, in true eighteenth-century style the purpose of the evening is for the punters (under ideal circumstances they would all be friends of the host and, to be fair, many are) to talk a bit, sniff the flowers, walk round the lake, eat well and be entertained by music. All is immaculate in the swagger portrait way. This sounds unkind, critical, but it is not. I feel the eighteenth century translated to the twentieth, and report what I sense.

The opera starts at the most unusual time. *Death in Venice* begins at 5.50, planned in order that the first Act will finish for dinner at seven-ish. There follows an interval of one hour, fifteen minutes.

Here I must stop, put on my costume and sing the first Act. I have already spoken of the role at length, but it must be emphasised that Aschenbach is a vocal and emotional marathon. To run this course nine times in about three weeks needs reserves of physical power which sometimes I feel I don't possess. I consider myself to be an intellectual and physical sprinter, an easily bored explosive eventer, with little interest or gift for endurance. This is changing, perforce.

Well, the old hysterical weak breathlessness came on again. No one would have noticed, but it's not a pleasant experience feeling that a collapse is imminent. I made two small mistakes known only to the conductor and me. In fact it's been a fine first Act.

The remarks I made concerning the attitude to the commodity of the purchaser were made blazingly clear. A completely unnecessary cough on the line, 'Don't smile like that' shattered the carefully constructed tension. This was an ignorant action from a philistine. It is a piquant combination, this arrogant and ignorant meld. We have paid, so we can cough where and when we like. The man didn't cough again during the whole performance; I was listening for him.

This Glyndebourne interval is highly disturbing to a debutant like me. Having built up a considerable head of steam and with boiling blood (interesting mix this) careering around my veins, I'm faced with the need to keep up the level artificially by walking, talking and acting a general qui-viveness or by letting the adrenalin leak from my toes, soaking the nylon carpet and wetting the floorboards as it goes. I've decided on the second way and can even now feel my interest in the second Act waning. I've decided to wait for the half-hour call, look at the dots remaining and then work up the interest again. Meanwhile I'll stop writing, snoop at the punters from the long gallery window, come back and tell you what I saw.

The miracles of nature continue. Today, 13 July in Sussex might as well be 1 January in Antarctica. I'm sure I saw Scott leaving his tent, and as I stopped on my walk to the gallery a couple of huskies peed in my shoes. (Their names, by the way, were Fasolt and Faffner.) It's freezing and the skies are pouring with Niagaran intensity, yet I saw four people sitting at a table, candles bravely flickering, while champagne was being served and two servants (drivers I assumed) held enormous gold umbrellas over the joyous party. Others sat on the open soaking ground, determined not to be disappointed and their pleasures destroyed by the feckless heavens.

The women tend to dress in the most marvellously outmoded fifties' style, and look as if they are wearing curtains. I feel they hire this dreadful gear from distressed gentlefolk in Fulham shops. Fuchsia seems to be the predominant colour today. The men, mostly dressed in the tedious garment known as black tie, tend to hold the programmes and laugh in a braying style that denotes their ease in such surroundings. The gay chaps mince about, showing their contempt for the banker-straight class by wearing what they would like to think of as outrageous: e.g. the odd black shirt with white rhinestones, bootlace ties, gorgeous coloured vests, boots with generous heels. The peacocks peacock for the peacocks. It's all very touching.

Now the half-hour has been called. I must wind myself up again, turn the screw another notch, change into my second-half gear and dare the world again. Yes, again.

Cash Time

Singers are notoriously keen to receive their money. The thought of it buoys them through those duff shows with the execrable conductor, the stupid producer and the blind designer. The fee cossets them through succeeding years, providing them with the life they desire by the means that they don't necessarily love – namely singing. The fright of the next show is often pacified by the vision of the heavenly cheque floating tantalisingly out of reach, but which glides slowly nearer until it is grabbed and pocketed at the end of the performance.

This, I know, sounds monstrously pecuniary and it is an exaggeration. There is, however, a truth lurking in its heart. To singers the question of money is of such importance that they rarely speak of it. Singers will say: 'There's no money at Wigan but do try Heligoland.' For my own case, I will admit that I get paid four times as much for singing Monastotos in Spain than for singing in Munich and at Covent Garden. But as for declaring their personal fees, singers are as tight as virgin bearded clams in June. The reasons for this trait are easy to find.

First, you don't want your nearest rival to know that you are twice as cheap as he is; under such circumstances you will appear an under-cutting swine, a goalhanger, a bit of a cheap slut. Second, should the amount of fees be general knowledge, the bottom fee would probably become the norm and the profit of some would plummet. A similar argument concerning standardisation of fees has recently been discussed by the opera intendants. Had the plan been effected, Glyndebourne and Madrid would pay the same singer the same fee. In this case Glyndebourne would lose badly and could not pay the inevitably larger fee, as it is not subsidised by the government. This state of monetary affairs would pertain generally, as each national opera is awarded different state grants.

Some houses would gain, but most would lose. Standardisation, too, could never benefit the highly successful star. As most starlets have huge ambitions for ascension to the big league, they could not compromise their egos with the acceptance of a set fee. So fees are secret. *Omertà* is the abiding principle of singers and their money.

Having touched on the ego, I will explain a little more. As mentioned previously, the ego is so easily shattered that it must be kept in a small bag of edible velvet with satin ties that massage it at every twitch and whinny. Should it realise that another – to it, a less accomplished artist – was getting double its fee, the pyschological blow would be so great that it would die. So it keeps stumm and continues the game.

Most singers get paid by banker's draft, cheque or cash. 'Cash?' I hear you gasp with incredulity.

'Yes,' I answer. Some money is still paid in greasy readies.

In Germany the cashier will always appear at the interval of the opera, brown paper envelopes in hand. You sign a paper to say you've received it and then worry what you are going to do with it for the second part. (By paying at the interval the financial management are keeping an old tradition – more of this later – and it also means that the staff don't have to wait for curtain down.)

I deal with this excess of cash in two ways. At the first costume fitting I usually ask whether a pocket or two won't completely ruin the designs. Often they don't, and with such pockets the money problem is solved. I wonder how many people have noticed me walking with a distinct bias in the second half of the show. There is also the possibility of leaving the cash with the dressers, i.e. those who help us get dressed – surprise, surprise. This I only do after I have given them a silent but stringent character analysis. The country in which one is singing also must be taken into consideration – not that I am xenophobic, but one can't be too careful.

There are some singers who have off-shore company bank accounts. In this case the money will be transferred directly, usually with no tax withheld. Other artists prefer the cheque to be paid directly into their bank. This can take anything from four days to three weeks. My own penchant is for cash.

I believe most strongly that cash in the hand is worth two in the post.

Some countries still have strict regulations as to how much cash can be taken out. This has led to many a riotous, skulldugger situation. Also, the unsavoury places in which cash has been secreted would bring a blush even to the most experienced of bearded clams. I remember trying to walk normally through Charles de Gaulle Airport in Paris with cash in my socks and more cash in my shoes. Every step made a deafening sound, a little as if I was running over a field of Rice Krispies or tearing through a wood in late autumn.

Now, more of the reasons why some managements still pay at the interval. The answer, I believe, is to be found in the history of performance practice.

Picture the scene. The month is July, the country Lower Saxony, the year 1680. I'm (remember me?) Max Hughescoq, sitting quietly at the clavichord – what else can you do with such an instrument, I hear you scoff – improvising and with luck (or might it have been divine providence?) inventing the toccata when I hear a knocking at my door. I hear, quite distinctly,   /0 and wonder whether the same providence requires readmission. I open the door and see standing before me – with some hauteur, it must be said, and wearing a magnificent scarlet-gold footman's costume – a servant of the Grossherzog of Tief-Püsschen. He hands me a letter, written on the highest-quality parchment, and in a fine non-committal hand rather reminiscent of later copperplate. (You will understand that Max is a bit of a time traveller.) The tenor of the communication?

I had been asked, nay commanded, to organise a concert of my music on 21 July at the Schloss, in the great hall. This is exciting news. A retrospective in my comparative youth! They must think highly of me. I lose no time and send a runner to the members of the Hughescoq ensemble, to wit Heinrich Camp, first fiddle, Muschi Schwartz, flute, Conrad Schvul, oboe, Angelika Dyke, viola da braccia, Sappho Diesel, viola da gamba, and Guillaume de Nancy on brass. I receive, by the returning quick feet, the glad news that all are free and whimpering for work. My mind, as swift as the bite of a mongoose, goes to work. (I have an agent, Lesbia Stier, but decide to keep her out of this one.)

Yes, I've chosen to sing in both halves to vary the sound a little. The interval, I'm told, is going to be interestingly long because the snouts will be down and the trotters in. I finish the programme. It's gorgeous, mixed and quite winsome. There are enough sad numbers to let the punters know that we're not patronising them, and enough quick and charming ones for them to really like and discuss in their knowledgeable tones.

The day of 21 July is one of those wondrous creations which demands my soul. It sucks me in, relieves me of those feelings of useless separation. My skin becomes malleable, a continuing of all skins, rinds, barks, feathers, scales. With difficulty and brutality I detach myself from this breathless unity. I wrench myself from the arms of infinity and prepare for work.

We arrive. The door is opened and I meet the Grossherzog Langendik of Tief-Püsschen. He is an urbane man, cool and so in charge that had a rampaging buffalo charged into the room he would have offered it a glass of sack. We are led to our rooms – I think they might more properly be called quarters – through moley subterranean passages with walls exuding a sticky green film. As musicians we naturally find ourselves guided to the servants' area. The commodity principle is in full spate here. The rehearsal is excellent, each musician keeping something back for the show. This especially applied to me – I had sung too many great performances away in rehearsal.

The concert is an enormous, popular success; and after, as is my wont, I go to the comptroller of the household finances. (I forgot to mention that I had previously arranged a heavyish fee for the group, out of which I was to keep 50 per cent.) He looks discomfited and slightly embarrassed – only slightly of course, because he is an excellent aper of his master's sangfroid – and tells me that there is no money.

'What do you mean, no money?' I say most shirtily. 'We have a verbal contract.'

He tries to mollify me: he tells me that the money has been previously invested in the cause of scientific discovery. Evidently a certain Professor Hans Hundsfott has been studying – with some vigour – the forms, various shapes and sizes and varied habitat of the common bearded clam. I will be paid, of course I will be paid, have no fear.

Truth to tell, I did receive the money three years later. My future contracts were written and included a clause stipulating that the cash was to be received at the interval. No spondulicks, no second half.

Such a story explains the now curious custom of payment at the interval in cash.

No Cash Time

In my now extensive experience, I have only been welched on once. This is not a verb that I love inordinately, as it is too close to my nationality to be madly humorous. The history of this debt is most interesting. I will tell you and instruct the young. About ten years ago I received an invitation to sing at a stately home in Surrey. The owner, a man of immense girth weighing in at at least thirty stone, was also clearly a man of huge greed. His name was Billy Bigster or something close to it. Entering the estate, we found the house surrounded by Ramboid body guards, rottweilers and the occasional daring sparrow. Each of the cold-eyed killers toted a carbine. This is not a usual scene for simple Schubert-toting musicians and we found it amusing, if not quite alarming.

The once elegant and I'm sure immaculate gardens were now littered with Moores, Hepworths, Caros, Frinks and other luminary sculptors (all of which were on loan, I was later informed). I must say these artists are brave indeed when they exhibit in the open air, in fields and gardens. Not only do they look immeasurably tatty and down at heel, but they take on a battle they cannot win. When you challenge the infinite art of the sycamore or oak you must be an imbecile, a supreme egoist or a masochist. I know of a Henry Moore that squats among the splendours of the Dart Valley. It has all the charm of the turd in the punchbowl. But I digress.

We were shown to our rooms – not, it must be said, the servants' quarters this time. The start of the recital was delayed while the elephant entered; his seat was a large sofa, his slim, elegant wife finding no place on it. I performed in an extremely moderate way, my heart for some unknown reason being stubbornly absent.

Concerning this absence of heart I must quote Thomas Wright, who in 1604 reminded his actors of the way in which they could persuade an audience of their points:

> Cicero expressly teaches that it is almost impossible for an oration to stirre up a passion in his auditors, except he be first affected with the same passion himself . . . If we intend to imprint a passion in another, it is requisite first to be stamped in our hearts: for through our voices, eyes and gestures, the world will pierce and thoroughly perceive how we are affected. And for this cause the passion which is in our breast must be the fountain and origin of all external actions; and as the internal affection is more vehement, so the external persuasion will be more potent . . . The actions of the bodies should be, in a perfect persuader, an image of the passion in the mind . . . And in the substance of external action for most past orators and stage players agree.

So do singers. This is exactly the reason for the poor performance. As I said before, my heart wasn't in it. The concert over, the host insisted on having his picture taken with us – not a pleasant experience. The work completed, I forgot that the recital had ever happened and took on more interesting tasks.

Two months or so later, I noticed in the press that a certain Mr Bigster – an Englishman – had been arraigned in America for some fearful felony and been incarcerated for debt and other minor infringements. The debt, I believe, was in the region of £50 million, the sentence endless.

At about the same time, I asked my agents whether the Surrey fee had arrived. The answer, naturally enough, was negative. Thinking that it was the manager who was responsible for collecting my fee, I asked him to move his butt and get it. He told me that agents are not responsible for the collection of fees. The law does not allow it. The artist alone is the one to chase good and bad debts. For years I had believed this not to be the case, for years seen fee after fee being paid into the bubbling bank accounts of the agent and staying there for months earning the interest which was rightly mine. I had been wrong. Quite shocked, I felt that I had been misled. From that moment, also, I decided that I alone would garner the fruit of my labour. As to the fee – what chance did I have of claiming my pittance while others fought for millions? And answer came there: 'None.' I mention this story for the benefit of the young who believe that agents have a power which they do not possess.

Managers or Agents

Having spoken of managers and agents, perhaps I should go on. This has always been a difficult and perplexing area for young singers. If I explain this morass in the life of a warbler, they may be helped. So how does a modern singer get a manager and, if lucky, how does he relate to him (or her). The answer is, I think, by luck. He (or she, naturally) may have sung well in the opera at the conservatoire at the end of term; on the other hand he (or she) may well have been in fiercely awful voice sounding like a dyspeptic kitten. He might now have a prestigious prize, yet again he probably does not. Had he been successful, a manager might well have noted him and asked to meet him. The young artist might have written to an agent, might have received an answer – but probably would not. As you see, it's all a bit of a gamble. If he could have been personally recommended by a well-respected musician that would have been good. But what great musician would know him? He is still in his tadpole phase.

Let us assume that, by any of these fortunate chances, he finds himself with an agent. He will then begin to ask questions to this most important middleman. He will expect a career to be created for him. He wishes to be turned from a frog into a prince, from a pauper to a millionaire. If these things fail to materialise – and they almost certainly will – he will begin to wonder what agents do. We should now discuss this.

An agent or manager is the person who brings the consumer and the commodity together. For this service he will expect a fee, called commission, of between 15 and 20 per cent. For his part, ideally, he will be expected to know what repertoire is being planned in the opera houses and concert halls of the world. He will be part of a network of managements. An artist often has a world representative – he who leases him for a smaller commission to various foreign agents. With his knowledge of repertoire and of his artist, he will be expected to use his judgement to place the artist ideally, to their mutual benefit. Thus a career might be planned and the singer – with a fair wind – proceed to a healthy retirement in perhaps his early to middle sixties. He can continue so long because, with the perfection of the planned life and with roles exactly suitable, his constitution and instrument will never have been unduly strained.

There is some truth in this pre-planned scenario, and some singers have indeed had such careers. More often, however, the truth is more haphazard and flawed. The one self-evident truth is that the agent is only as good as his material. Should a singer find himself asking why he is not getting more work, and then blaming his agent for the paucity, he is kidding himself. A manager can do nothing with fourth-rate goods. Artists always get themselves work. If this is the case, one might genuinely and reasonably ask what the percentage is paid for. The answer to this is that agents are not only the finders and organisers of work, they also provide 'services'. Good managers will provide travel and accommodation, a secretarial service, general and sometimes specific psychological pampering. A personal secretary would demand far more for similar services.

The problem with agencies (providing you have a good talent) is that, like almost everything, as they get older and more successful they tend to lose their virility, becoming greedy and self-capon-content. Also, a singer will do well to bear in mind that, unless he is one of the very highest money-earners in the world, his contribution in commission will only pay for one of the agency's assistants – and they are pitifully paid. These secretary/PAs tend to be well-bred girls just down from university – usually Oxbridge – and are desperate to get a job. The world of the arts is full of such people. With their English degrees they descend on the world's publishing houses, art houses and music agencies as leaves fall in autumn. They find the work seductive, especially mixing with the celebrities. They have too little experience of the commercial world to demand too much for their labour.

So the average singer brings to the expanding agency very little indeed. The big money is to be found in management fees. Festivals are large earners, as are touring orchestras. It is only too easy for the agent to lose sight of his burgeoning singer under the weight of commission deposited by the Vienna Philharmonic.

Having asserted that a 'planned career' is not possible in most cases I must tell what usually happens, the more pragmatic way.

The phone rings. It's your agent.

'Hey, Max, I've got an enquiry for '97.'

'Hello, Dick, what is it?'

(This Dick, by the way, is not the Richard de la Tête of the castle. I believe, however, I am the Max in the same scene.)

'A revival of the new piece you did for Munich five years ago. Interested?'

This is the moment of truth. This moment always occurs and will always be answered differently by every singer. The thoughts flashed through me in an order not too distant from this. The piece, let me think about the piece, was it too difficult, too demanding? The memory roars back. It remembers the hideous set, extremely difficult make-up with an enormous pear-shaped head which was uncomfortably heavy. The costume was huge, also mighty heavy, encumbering. The production was extremely lively for me. Up and down ladders, carrying guns, running around; I remembered it all too well. The piece was Krysztof Penderecski's *Ubu Rex*. The music marvellous, cynical, ironic with glorious sick tunes in F and B♭ major. It was an extraordinarily clever score. My part – Ubu – was a masterpiece for a singer-actor, which most people think I am. I remember it as hard work but seriously rewarding – a part in the Loge, Herod stable.

I would be about fifty-eight, just about possible for such an athletic jaunt (I've always had a horror of dying for any cause – especially the stage). I can do it, but as I'm lazy I don't want to. But a voice questions me – no, informs me.

'But it's work, *work*. You remember – the thing that you've been doing for thirty-three years. Remember, too, what it does for you.'

'What does it do?' I feebly question myself.

'It prevents you from seeing your obsessions for what they really are.'

'What are they?'

'They are the fripperies of a bored, spoilt man. You don't need any of them, but they make your life interesting. Consider real necessities and the spirit in whose hand you doze!'

'What's the fee, Dick?' I'm back to reality.

'Oh, we'll play for a rise of . . .' (Remember the chapter on fees.)

'Oh, why not? I know it,' I say. Immediately I see the loss of beard and the lack of home for at least a month.

'Shall I take it, then?'

'Yes, why not?'

Such is the planning of a career. There may be some who have enough blatant love of themselves to say no and no again until a role is offered which they consider good enough for them, for their self-image. I cannot do this; my temperament will not allow it. Their attitudes I call hubris and mine cowardice. But we understand ourselves – or at least I hope we do.

Rehearsals

I'll wander now into the world of the rehearsal room. Some rehearsals can be illuminating and exciting, others so moribund that life seems to stop every second a year. How does the singer deal with the ineffable tedium of the latter? On a purely practical level I would advise a digital watch. By turning all the fixtures to zero, time is abolished and you won't find yourself constantly watching the clock. But I will explain the kind of scene that the singer might find.

The director or conductor who is the motivator of your bowel-concreted boredom is not necessarily bad or incompetent or even nasty. All that has occurred is that your personalities are so dissimilar as to be mutually exclusive, your temperaments so distant that there can be no point of contact. I remember being invited by the Salzburg Festival to sing Don Basilio in their production of *Figaro*. I would have to spend one month rehearsing a piece which I had sung over a hundred times.

(Before I continue with this I must quickly tell of the genesis of this engagement. Three years earlier, when they were casting for *Figaro*, I kept running into a sentence. It was: 'You haven't met Maestro Karajan yet.' This was far from the truth, as twenty years earlier I had sung for him, been offered Froh in his *Ring* at the Metropolitan, New York. I had turned it down and was told, 'If you don't want to sing for me, Herr Tear, goodbye.' Nevertheless the sentence was repeated as if on a loop. I soon discovered that 'meet' was a euphemism for 'audition'.

'When I meet Karajan, what shall I do?'

'Oh, take a bit of Don Basilio with you and you can discuss.'

To cut a long story painfully short. I turned up at the Grosses Festspielhaus at lunch on a Sunday – that time when decent people have recently returned from the pub and are scoffing their roast beef, roast potatoes, Yorkshire pudding and cabbage in England. There he was, sitting far at the back behind a console of NASA-like proportions, like the Mekon waiting to destroy Dan Dare. A voice croaked through the PA system.

'Could you sing a little of Basilio, Herr Tear? Begin with the first récit.'

I began: *'Susanna il ciel vi salvi.'*

I was stopped.

'Thank you, Herr Tear, that is excellent.'

Such is power and such is the system. On with the rehearsal.)

The six weeks I'm to spend in Austria will be spent in physical comfort, I shall be in luxury, supplied by God's own mountains and his own choice of best weather – witheringly hot days, punctured (mercifully usually, and thoughtfully, at dead of night) by shattering thunderstorms.

The festival has decided, with the wisdom of its own egoism, that the usual three-hour rehearsal session is not enough and must be lengthened by forty-five minutes. For the habituated obsessional like me this is all too much. The extra three-quarters of an hour would be to me excessive even were the conditions ideal, i.e. a director of penetrating interest, with charm, wit and wisdom overflowing. Although the director is a niceish and competent man, this is not the case.

All the cast have performed their roles many times before. It is usual that, although you try to be quite open-minded, you tend to bring some ideas to a new production. These have generally seeded themselves from the best productions you have been in. Thus all new productions tend to have pieces of others within them. The work that appeals and sticks is the one closest to your temperament; for new ideas to erase the old, they have to be very good indeed. These were not.

It is always enlightening when one arrives at a rehearsal, whether concert or opera, and hears no music being rehearsed. Rather, one hears the voice of the conductor or producer/director speaking with confidence and authority. I feel the blisters of my boredom beginning to smart. I know instinctively that the director/conductor feels he is an everything manqué. I inwardly howl with pain knowing that his accomplishment – energy, interest, attraction, riches, way with women, vocabulary, languages are all lost desires which mask a hole within him that he cannot fill. He whistles into his soul and the vacuum echoes his tunes.

This time he will try to do something 'new' with *Figaro*. My heart sinks. No more can be done with either ideas or tempo. We can muck about with set and sound, but nothing 'new' will be discovered. Man can only go so far in interpreting that conceived by man. I'm going to have to stand this for one whole month. A month watching a man, a posture, a show-off, assert his authority, invent brilliant solutions, while my brain is always an hour ahead of his.

I know what he's going to say next. It's all so predictable. Yes, here it comes.

'I've been thinking, Max. I want Don Basilio to be all watching and oily!'

'Really? What a brilliant idea, I hadn't thought of that!' The stars judder to a stop, the firmament shrieks: 'Yes, oh yes, oh yes.'

'A new vision, we will reverse,' say the planets. On and on it goes, cardboard thought followed by plastic gesture.

I sign off, of course. This is the only thing to do. I bring down the shutters, say yes, of course, what a good idea, knowing that I will always do it my way. This is where the watch comes in. When all the numbers are at nought, I adopt a Zen master's stillness. The world proceeds sensibly and the idiocies of the producer don't touch me. This attitude is not as negative as it might seem. The recharging of over-tired batteries is tangible. The watchful calm I have assumed leads me to that essential area which is so necessary if I am going to have all my colours and possibilities. This area might be called the dimension of eternity. With this vision I can see many things, but from a point much farther off or out. It gives me a healthy perspective of events and reduces my own ego to that famous grain of sand that lodged itself under Blake's toenail.

Clearly each must make his own way with this problem of the dire rehearsal period. It is worth bearing in mind that most of the people in power over us are spurred in the need to control by a lack of understanding of themselves, and usually also by a lack of spiritual vision.

I hinted earlier that conductors are no innocents in this ego maelstrom. You will be encouraged to sing in a more relaxed way, feel, mine passion, sing higher, deeper, lower, softer, lighter, louder by a man who has no voice, no conception of the technique needed to produce a product of evenness and beauty and line, but only a desire to do what you are doing. Each poor player and singer will be encouraged, activated to the maestro's vision, that glorious, unique thing which that too-loved boy possesses. Each will have to temper his own-born-uniqueness for another's. This other desires his temperament to be seen as awesome, God-inspired. Under such considerations, it's small wonder that conductors have such a hard time of it.

When I 'sign off' from a dim director, the babble, the madness nevertheless continue. It is well to remember that the ear of the stage director is only just past its zenith. The wheels of his desire still turn. Even now he batters at the intendant's door with yet more demands.

'I cannot see it until it's built,' comes the spoilt cry. When it is built the cry changes.

'It's rubbish,' he says. 'Let's start again. And thousands on thousands of money – better spent elsewhere – is channelled again into a creation in which the music should always have dominated.

Even now they are demanding five months' rehearsal for *The Magic Flute*. Who is going to pay poor Monostatos for his time? They will include an extra two fees for rehearsals. What we are watching is the exercising of two huge faults. The first is rampant egoism with its need for power and control, the second that you can organise tomorrow from today. This mad ride of the director must be stopped, he must be harnessed, he must be made to see his function which is to be one cog in a great wheel. His tame cat, his familiar, the dramaturg must also look for work elsewhere. A dramaturg is the intellectual justifier of the director. These so-called intellects attempt to explain the story and its dramatic and psychological aspects to extremely sharp people who have already worked it all out for themselves.

Touring with Süssmayr

Touring is an interesting phenomenon. All musicians must tour. Ever since the medieval Minnesingers the performer has spent at least five months a year on the road. This style of life can cause considerable shock. It needs to be thought out and, once understood, rigorously acted upon. Can you imagine this unrest of travel, of being away, of not being surrounded by those loved practical objects by which we judge our time, in which we feel stupidly comfortable and without which we are deracinated and threatened? So we must come to terms with the void in which we must live and the void within which prompts in us such thoughts.

Should this be achieved, touring can be amusing and illuminating. There is always time, and this must be filled. I will give you an example. (Also, when touring, you tend to perform the same piece ten to twenty times, which gives plenty of time for reflection on the nature of the piece in question.) Follow me. I'll begin with a touring story.

Touring is a living area for the musician. The act of selling one's artistic wares to foreign parts fulfils two functions. First, much money is made by the artists and managers, and second, goodwill flourishes with the possible outcome of more tours and perhaps economic endeavours in other fields. A tour can be undertaken with anything from a string quartet, madrigal group or solo singer to a symphony orchestra with soloist or a chamber orchestra with choir. In this last case, a well-recorded and good-selling band brings with it its own choir, which usually consists of a group of amateur (highly educated) singers.

The combination and accumulation of this band of singers is not so important to this tale. The members of London's amateur choirs are those who are either hoping to make a professional career (not many, it must be admitted) or who while at university sang madrigals, the odd Verdi *Requiem* and *B Minor Mass* for fun, and then on leaving university went into the teaching fraternity or joined the banking world and found in their chosen careers that they dearly missed singing. At some time they married people in a similar position. They are well-educated and liberal people. Some lack the passion that love was told to demand. They feel warmish about things, happyish, comfortablish, but notice a dullness at home. Bread is constantly placed on bread without noticeable friction. Good manners and politeness can bow themselves stiff. Priapus might have been ignored. Madame Vag. feels an emptiness.

The orchestra, on the other hand, is usually a band of talented, professional journeymen, playing town by town in a gum-chewing, poker-playing classical rodeo, with a 'Bring on the pieces, we'll ride 'em' attitude. Here is a potentially explosive situation. Hard, chewing men are about to meet a group of sensitive, caring, emotionally deprived *pucelles*. The strain of the manacled libido shrieks.

The meeting at Heathrow would be a joy for sexual sociologists. The sight is filled with nods, becks and smiles and murmurs under a heavy breath of 'I'm a married woman, I'm here for Wolfgang', 'I can't wait to see the fake Frans Hals', 'I feel guilty about leaving the children with that incompetent nanny', then 'Oh! it'll be good for them.'

The plane takes off and decorum is maintained. Those designated to share rooms begin to make contact with like or dislike. The orchestra waits with the patience of celibate vultures. Comes the landing, and as if by magic comes fraternisation. Down come the borders and the drawers.

The first night is interesting, especially if you are fortunate enough or even unfortunate enough to be next door to a lust liaison. Perils of aircraft, hurricanes, tornados put aside, head is now on pillow and there is no difference between the mattress and you. Suddenly, as if in a dream, come sounds of pain; quiet groans pierce the cocooned comfort. Awakened state is sharp. What is this mounting moaning from next door? These are no sounds of pain but of pleasure, an alto is reaching the gates of heaven. The night then becomes a staccato of shrieks, murmurs, giggles and the pattering of slipperless hooves. Shouts answer shouts, whinnies are heard, cocks crow, out of the slips and bras for England and abroad.

This story defeats itself in repetition for a week, the late Sunday breakfast the only clue as to who did what with whom. Guilt covers muesli; downcast, sad eyes beckon forgotten partners in the dull sixties' rooms out of sight. Lust will reawaken soon, but now is the quiet remorse of memory. I watch these liaisons with equanimity, a certain pleasure and a damaged hand cut when my listening glass shattered.

Why this scene happens more with amateurs than pros I can only guess, suspecting that those being paid for doing a job don't expect to enjoy themselves. For those of less libidinous leisures I'm sure that the tour provides not only good friendship but also shared and heavy musical love.

I'm constantly amazed by the fifth-form humour that haunts my brain. I find it seriously funny, though I don't know why it should be so. When I read an article written without tongue in cheek declaring that Mr Prick achieved a tremendous climax in the last Act of *Tristan*, that Mr Cuenod's cock was outstanding, that Mr Vickers must change the spelling of his name when he sings in Germany, then I'm tickled. Joy of supreme joys, this morning I see on a hoarding a bass announced with the most marvellous name of Prickwinkel – talk about gilding the lily. How long is eternity?

My previous discussion of touring also has a more serious side. As a member of such excursions one generally performs the same piece night after night. In so doing, the piece becomes familiar. Some survive this treatment of familiarity, others don't.

In a similar way that nine consecutive performances of Britten's *War Requiem* showed the sticking plaster and weaknesses of the choral writing, so seven shows in eight days of the Mozart *Requiem* have given me new intuitions (and they are only these) of the story of its composition. I became aware of such a unity of utterance as performance followed performance that I was forced to think again of the origins of the Requiem. I became surer by the bar that the piece was all from Mozart's hand. The strength not only of composition but also of inspiration is manifest throughout the work and has drawn me to a hypothesis.

As I am clearly no academic, and as sometimes certain ideas are best told as stories, I will use this form.

You perhaps are not aware of that hot scene with Elvira Madigan that Mozart conducted with such finesse. Well, his wife Constanze heard about it and wasn't pleased. In order to partake of the gander sauce she has availed herself of a lover, one Francis Xavier Süssmayr. Constanze, not a forgiving girl, has watched the failing health and then the death of her husband with mixed emotions. There is an imperative hanging over her. The manuscript of the *Requiem* is complete (with the exception of the last movement); it is essential that it be delivered to Count Walsegg-Stuppach at his home, Schloss Stuppach, near Wiener Neustadt in the southern part of lower Austria. The hundred ducats are in the bank, the ink is almost dry, the funeral is a matter of days away.

As if with a camera we trace our path up three flights of stairs to a rather large gold room, number 31 of the Moser Hotel in Baden. The room has seen easier days. The wallpaper is detaching itself, the paint around the door-lock is chipped with the many misses of keys in dark shadows. Against the wall on the left side of the room there is a bed on which rest two forms. The verb here is ill chosen. It is inappropriate. No rest is apparent. In this crumpled, dirty-looking bed, a man and woman are making love. The bed shudders with their ecstasy, the room – very resonant with stone floors and walls – echoes to their cries. A chamber pot under the bed is half-full, a standard black poodle with reddish eyes in the corner understands exactly the state of play.

If we wait a few minutes – looking aside for pure decency – we may well learn something.

'Oh, Frank, that was absolutely wonderful, as always.'

Frank said nothing, reaching instead for a leather pouch full of tobacco. He began to fill his meerschaum pipe. When it was full of tobacco he lit it deliberately. He turned to the woman, whose name was Constanze, his face filled with sadness, the dark flower of his heavy mind.

Constanze continued, partly to relieve his gloom, partly to reassure herself: 'What *is* the matter, my love? You look so woebegone. Is it that you don't love me any more? Or is it that since Wolf's death sex is no longer exciting, that I'm no longer desirable?'

Twilight was possessing Austria, the room darkened, the shadows assumed weight. With the darkening of nature, so Frank's features became ever more heavy.

'No, my darling,' he said. 'The problem is not yours, rather it is mine. As an artist and a man I am a hopeless failure.'

Connie stopped him, putting her fingers to his lips. She said: 'Sweetheart, I love you. I've had enough of living with a genius, with its difficulties and constant betrayals. No woman could have borne it as well as I: chronic money problems, infidelities with people in the theatre, with colleagues, with pupils. It's been a nightmare. The last of his affairs almost drove me to suicide.'

'Which was that, Con?' said Frank.

'Oh! I must have told you.'

'No, you didn't,' Frank said almost impatiently. 'Tell me!'

'It concerned a woman called Magdalena Hofdemel,' said Connie. She continued: 'She went to Wolfy for piano lessons and of course, yes, naturally, the inevitable happened. Soon it was discovered that she was pregnant. Her husband the civil servant Franz found out, not only about her pregnancy, but also who the possible father was, and the sweet musical liaisons, and beat her unmercifully. Oh! I forgot to mention that this Franz Hofdemel was, like Wolfy, a mason. Anyway, one day after Wolfgang's death on 6 December, Hofdemel committed suicide.' Here Connie paused for breath, stroked Süssmayr's hair and attempted to draw him to her.

'Can you imagine the scandal!' she said. 'There was talk of poisonings and masonic intrigues. There were rumours of friends, masonic friends, gathering together to try and diffuse a scandal in the brotherhood. Even I believed that *they* were responsible for his pauper's burial, so that there would be less scandal. These things don't bother me now. I loved him – of course I loved him. Who would not love a man of such energy, intellect, life? Who wouldn't have died for such passion? Then, my dearest, it became too much. I was a singer, a good singer, but I was also a woman. I couldn't stand his unfaithfulness. I had and have my inborn truths which no man might share. Frank, when I knew you wanted me and courted me, I could not resist – no woman can resist such endeavour, such fervour. I became yours, and love to be so.'

Darkness had won its daily battle. In order to see the beautiful face of Frank, Constanze left the bed and lit a solitary candle which stood on the only table, next to the bed. It cast shadows of intrigue and drama. Noses cast the shadows of bodies, intuitions became religious, and feelings whispered in Greek. The candle brightened as the dark deepened. The poodle renounced its interest and slept – seeming to be engaged in an unfathomable race with pigeons and leather leads.

'Oh, Connie, what can I do?'

Frank kissed Con again, sucking in her lower lip. He gently stroked her belly. Sex took its course.

Two and a half hours later, sitting in a fine old inn on the east side of Baden, the two looked a happy, easy pair, but all was not necessarily as it seemed. The building was comfortably warm. The roof was barrel-vaulted. Wood panelling rose three-quarters of the way up the walls while above pouted carved putti, bunches of easily entwining grapes and predictable corn stooks. The light, a twittering candlepower that enhanced smell, beauty and thought, threw its warm silk on the two who sat, drank, ate, considered and spoke.

'Darling, the fact is that you are *not* a genius, not a great composer – you are a good, workaday journeyman artist and none the worse for that. You simply have to admit this, or life will become even more impossible. Genius is selective and destructive. I have tasted it and I don't need it. Genius descends from heaven like a bolt, and strikes unsuspecting brains where it descends and lights forever on the shoulder and screams its commands.'

Connie was getting bored with this whole question of Frank's gift.

'Always remember I love you. I love you for your kind, thoughtful, loving self.'

'That is quite enough for me on one level,' said Frank, 'but there's that terrible, empty, aching pain I suffer when I think how ordinary I am as a composer, an artist.'

The silence between them grew, as did the noise of the other diners. Each guffaw and shriek from that noisy table in the corner (they must have been actors) made the silence between the couple more complete.

As if to ease the tension, and out of habit, Frank reached into his pocket for his pipe and tobacco pouch. He drew them moodily from the right-hand pocket of his brown velvet coat, and as he did so a small scrap of paper fell to the floor.

Connie noticed and said: 'Frank, look, you've dropped something. What is it?'

'I've absolutely no idea,' said Frank, picking up the paper.

He slowly opened out the crumpled object and smoothed it flat. It was a dirty, fingered torn bit of music manuscript. There were one or two pencil marks on the lines, and the odd musical phrase was just discernible.

'What *is* that?' Con enquired again.

Frank replied: 'Oh! just a couple of ideas Wolfy dotted down while we were having a beer or two, it must have been about nine months ago. I might as well throw it away.'

He began to recrumple the paper in an absent-minded way when Connie took his hand, saying: 'No, don't do that. Let me see what the sketches are.'

She took the paper, stretched it out once again and began to read the music.

'Aren't these a few phrases from the *Requiem*? I'm sure they are, Frank.'

Frank glanced at the fragments.

'Yes, you might be right – he certainly used them in the completed score. He must have been thinking about it as we chatted and drank. But they're no use now. Throw them away – the piece is finished and there's no point in keeping rubbish.'

Constanze paused, clearly in thought. Then, with a quick birdy turn of the head, she said excitedly, 'Frank, I've got an idea!'

Frank continued in the old tempo, taking tobacco from his pouch, grass-seeded with flowery patterns. He said, without looking up, 'Well, tell me then.'

'What if . . .' She stopped, thought, then hesitatingly continued, 'What if I had an idea that could help you? How would that strike you?'

With pipe now alight and reflexes at the usual neutral, Süssmayr said: 'Go on, Con, go on.'

She did. 'You know you've always wanted to be seen as a great composer, and you know I've always loved you and wanted what you wanted. What if . . .' Again she stopped.

He, getting more interested, said (almost with passion): 'What if? Con! You can be slow.'

'What if we made out that *you'd* finished the *Requiem*? What if we showed just these pathetic scraps to the world? What if we went straight back home and threw away – no, burned – the complete manuscript? What if . . . we tried to say that as Wolfy died he gave you these scraps for you to complete, and you, dearest Franz, finished the whole score not only with Mozart's genius but also with an understanding that showed your complete love for the man? I loved him – Christ, of course I did – but I also love your calm, your honest fidelity. Love matters to me.'

Frank's interest was now keen. He listened with sharp ears and watched with ever-narrowing eyes.

Con continued. 'What d'you say, Franz?'

'I like it, Constanze,' he said. 'Who can know, who could discover? Even if I am still not regarded as a great composer, I will be seen as a friend (which I certainly was) and an extremely sensitive musician. Perhaps, if we do it, people will see my future efforts as more serious, more intellectual, more rational.'

Connie said, impulsively: 'Let's do it.'

The rest of the room had become quiet quite suddenly. The actors in the corner were drunk and hushed, the rest of the company prepared for home and sleep. Time had scythed by.

'Shall we walk?' she asked.

'Yes,' he replied with a slight note of guilt in his voice.

They returned home.

So it was performed. The full score was rewritten, the beautiful original dismembered and, with great sadness, quartered and burned. The scraps were kept as evidence of Franz's great skill.

Constanze and Franz *did* love each other.

The Coach

All through this assembling of ideas and aids for the young I'm troubled constantly that the world I express and see and of which I try to warn others is, of course, my own. Engels was his own perfect bourgeois when he commented on the condition of the working class in England. He saw what *he* saw and imagined *his* experience. He assumed their pain and disorder.

When writing, I can only achieve a similar end in this brutally solipsistic world. What I suppose I do is to purge my own sometime anger and frustration, and attempt to warn others with what are, after all, my own failings. I shall nevertheless continue to warn. To the young and sweet I offer another caveat. Don't take too easily to advice. Your blue blanket is defunct. I will explain.

> I say to you now, oh! my people: there are those who have
> failed who have not passed the test. Such people will come
> upon you as ravening dogs, as bees around the marmalade
> jar and as young scientists in quick search for the virgin
> bearded clam. They will assault your ears with so many
> wisdoms that you will scarce believe; offer such experiences,
> that will make the head of the bald sprout golden tresses
> in early spring; astound you with sleights of hand that far
> exceed the stick of Moses or the rod of Jesse: will curse you
> with ancient fearful stratagems and cabbalistic curses should
> you reject their words: and praise with such extravagance
> that the Veil will mend invisibly – if you show your need
> of them.

These people are the dispossessed, those excluded from the success they deemed rightly theirs, those who now are only allowed to eat the crumbs cast from the banquet called talent – and then quickly to avoid the flying feet. These are the ones who belch out the undigested hurt of *temps perdu.*

Such an excess gladly farted from the vent of this poet manqué, I shall now discuss the above (excessively referred to) – namely coaches, musical and verbal.

Now when I was a lad the only coach I knew was the one who hied my quaking self to away rugby and cricket fixtures, or the one in which, vainly, I tried to trap that Hilly object of my lust. Nowadays the noun 'coach' has appropriated more magus-like qualities, shamanistic echoes. From music to sport, the coach has appeared as the intercessor between the imaginary and the real, or as a priest to guide you through the fearful valley before you see God's face. The coach is experience that cannot give experience; the one who can explain the frying pan but not the spitting head lying in the boiling oil. I will not speak of teaching now – that may come later, and is a quite different product of a different union from a different egg. No, coaches certainly don't teach – they dispense vision and hard (I might even say hardly) acquired knowledge. Visualise this scene. Follow me.

I have been learning – they now say studying – a song by a certain Franz Schwanz-Kopf. Translated loosely (very loosely) from the German into French (Schwanz-Kopf's mother was French; he wrote the song in a small peasant village called Paix du Cul) it is called 'Le pauvre gentilhomme sans les valseurs'. It is a song of expressionistic winsomeness and painful charm. I have my own natural reaction to the music and words. I see it as an essentially light, ironic, not to say comic song about a poor meek man without any noticeable sadness who is nevertheless crippled with the growing insecurity that, as he approaches the cusp of senility, his testosterone level will fall and he will find himself a eunuch in all but two respects. This little, preposterous tale I viewed with a natural humour and scepticism and I was therefore prepared to sing it in an airy – not to say queenie – way.

To get to Heinrich Prick's house involved a rather tortuous journey to north London – a walk to Goldhawk Road station on the Metropolitan Line, a wait of twenty minutes (probably another insensitive suicide at the Barbican), a limping journey through tedious graffiti all written in the same copperplate *de nos jours*, on through Royal Oak (not another tree Charles I pissed upon) to Baker Street, then a change. I arrived, ten minutes late and in not too sound a mood. I rang a disconcerting chime and was bidden in. The rather cluttered room which housed the piano might have been from another century. Heavy, dirty, gold velvet curtains gasped for more dust, the worn Turkish carpet was littered with scores, papers, letters and rucked rugs. The piano, an ancient Bechstein (the kind that Liszt must have played) was covered with a dark red velour cloth. On this were old pictures in *Jugendstil* silver gilt frames. The people in them, I assumed, were the family members long since departed: uncles, aunts, mothers, fathers and early dead children were still fading sepia memoirs. There were two photographs – one of Schoenberg and one of Reger. They were both signed. In the same hand on each were the words 'with best wishes to the young Prick' signed separately by Arnold and Max.

The piano jangled in the strange way that pianos of the 1870s do. They sound as if they have ghosts in them, every note an echo of an older note, every tune a remembrance. So the piano jangled. Heinrich wheezed – too many cigarettes had clouded the tubes – and I sang; or at least I tried to sing, for before I had completed four bars he said: 'Vot do you sink you are doink?' With fury, he continued: 'You know nossink of zis *Lied*.'

I tried to explain my thinking but he would have none of it – he was far too practically Romantic for my cynicism. The damage was irreparable.

'Please tell me then what you think that it's about,' I said reasonably, and reasonably respectfully.

'I don't sink vat it's about!' he barked. 'I know vat it's about.'

'Then what is it about?'

'It is about – *aber* you're *zu jung* to understand – it is about ze sadness of age. Ze man can no longer to ze tea dances go. He can no more waltz *mit Lust*. Ze *Lied* is a metaphor – you say metaphor? Or is it a symbol? – for ze *temps perdu* and ze *Zukunft*.'

Which of us was correct could never be discovered; but I never sang that song again, my thinking being hopelessly compromised by his influence.

'Beware coaches!' comes my cry. Use what you know is useful to you, reject what is not and always resist the ego-power games. The truth, you will always find, is nearer to you than anyone else – nearer than you can ever expect.

Herod

Having spoken about the difficulties of singing and playing von Aschenbach at some length, I feel I should tell of another role: one which is special to me and one that up to this moment I have played over one hundred times. The role is that of Herod from the opera *Salome* by Richard Strauss.

It begins with a pink dress, grey overfolds added, a crown of roses, a ring for every finger and thumb, uncomfortable sandals. You are now ready, or at least you look ready.

A voice says: 'What about your inward state? How do you feel?'

'Well, not so bad really,' I answer; and continue, 'True, I've waited all day for this show, trying with vigour to think of other things but failing conclusively. Always the *Salome* peppers my thoughts.'

'What do you feel now?'

'Nothing much,' I answer, 'other than the notion that, during the forty minutes I must wait, some inward impulse forces me to walk. This old, old body must be activated – the blood must, as they say, course.'

'Have you warmed up?'

'No, not properly. If I give it too much before I get on I find the voice too light, too pretty. Yet, and now I understand your question, I do have to whack out a trumpety high line like *"Salome, komm trink Wein mit mir, einen köstlichen Wein"*, etc.'

'What do you do then?'

'Well, I give it enough warming to leave enough baritone in the sound, but not too much to turn me into a lyrical tenor, which I am . . . Don't ask any more questions – I won't answer them,' I add. Now I am left walking positively and fairly quickly with absolutely nowhere to go except the stage, which according to my ears won't need me for at least thirty minutes.

Once walking has woken my body up and the odd scale (always sung on the Ay vowel) has teased the voice into an acceptance of imminent combat, I am impatient to start.

Ten minutes to go. 'Oh, come on, call me!'

Nine minutes. *'Monsieur Tear, s'il vous plaît.'*

'Hi, Madame Hérodias, how are you?' (We meet at the door to the stage, the entrance to madness.) She, testing her voice mindlessly, says, 'Fine, thank you.' (My question too was meaningless, being voiced merely to lessen the tension.)

The time has passed, my time is come, Naraboth has killed himself. The music of the intermission that awaits the royal couple is nearly finished.

Herodias says with truth: 'The frogs now are mating – it must be time to go on.'

It *is* time to go on, and here I will cease this extremely silly scenario and comment only on the difficulty of singing and acting the part of Herod. Do not assume that my colleague and antagonist has ceased to exist. She hasn't; she has simply repossessed her own world which she would never have left had it not been for the exigencies of living (eating, getting to the theatre, etc.).

It's a blatant world that I walk into. The audience sits and listens or is bored. The lights themselves bore into my eyes and it's hard to see. I look towards the conductor and then look left, hoping to see Salome. *'Ah, da ist sie'* (Ah, there she is) is rendered with more than the relief of the actor.

Herod is a fascinating but one-dimensional character. Let me now consider what he is. Historically he is a quisling – a Jew who has sold out to the Romans and has been put in charge of the protectorate by way of thanks. This fact will render him a traitor to the nationalists and he will be on the hit list of the extremists. He must therefore be careful, must watch his step. This, so far, both he and his relations have been able to do. However, he is a Jew and as such is prey to Jewish traditions – the mystic traditions of the Hebrews. Thus it is a glory to die in battle but an impious and venial sin to kill a child in the womb (as they will provide men for a future army), or to leave the newborn for foxes. The stars, the sun and the moon will have their way. Herod is superstitious and political in that order. At the time he walks on to the stage he is guilty (having killed his brother) and also feeling the whip of second-class birth. Herodias, in her anger at his lust for Salome, reminds him in no uncertain terms that while he is the son of a camel-driver she is of royal blood. She in her magnanimity has married him and saved him from the breath and turds of his beasts.

He sees portents in the moon, he slips in blood, he wants his stepdaughter. Can madness be far away?

Strauss seems to have had a physical problem. First he asserts that conductors never should sweat (this surely is associated with the 'gentleman's' conduct of the time), then he asserts that Herod shouldn't rant and overplay the part – he assumes that the character of the unhinged will come across without gestures. (There could be more than a kernel of truth here. The music, however, tells me that this mental breakdown is physical and shows itself in physical madness.) Next time I will see how it works without unnecessary movement. My judgement is on ice. However, such a neurosis seems to demand a physical display. This is my present position.

There is no way that either the conductor's role or Herod's can be occupied without total belief. There is no standing off. The audience will notice nothing if you do not act and give with controlled vigour. An orchestra will play ordinarily if you don't take them by the balls with passion. (Sir Adrian Boult missed this one too.) Perhaps Edwardianism via its beliefs and physical manifestations was the opposite of the physical in its own manifestations. Perhaps unphysicality was the chic style of the time.

How therefore should Herod be played?

I think that at the start he must be played with a certain dangerous control. The audience must feel that madness or murder might happen at every instant. They are not disappointed when soon he has a guilt/panic attack and, throwing away his rosy crown, collapses frothing and panting.

For me it is a relief to throw away the crown, in which I feel remarkably silly. I've had about ten made for me and none has been to my taste. My taste would be to do away with the crown, turning it instead into part of his neurosis. But I accept that this is not likely to happen.

When he asks Salome to dance for him, much against the wishes of Herodias, he doesn't realise what the outcome will be but knows he is treading dangerous ground. He is so miserable, mad with misery, that he is willing to dare. It is almost the action of a suicide. He courts death. He feels death is near; he doesn't know whose death only that death will be the outcome.

Even when Salome promises to dance for him he is defeated. He has imagined that she will dance for him; instead she dances for John the Baptist. Her sexuality is fixed on the cistern. The consequence of Herod's stupid promise, *'Ich will sie dir alle geben'* – 'I will give you everything you ask for' – is mayhem.

During the dance Herod must be totally involved – remembering, however that he has his most testing section yet to sing, beginning, *'Ah, herrlich'* and then progressing with the utmost panic and speed. He offers her everything from jewels to peacocks, and finally the veil of the temple. She is adamant: she will take the head of the Baptist. He is now near collapse. He must pay. The head is severed and brought out. Herod becomes catatonically still.

This is a dangerous section in the singing of the part, for, although the body is dead in weight, it must be remembered that the fearfully difficult end, *'Man töte dieses Weib'*, with its $B\flat$ must be powerfully performed. The previous singing will have tried the

voice considerably and, while Salome is singing her long love song to the head, the voice will decide that its job is done. So Herod must be vocally but silently alert, and must not allow his tired body to dictate the terms.

The opera ends with three deaths, madness and a very dubious marriage.

So Herod is – so you are – finished. You are as exhausted as if you had run a marathon. Not much has happened to the character except that layers of hysteria have been put down with increasing speed. The actor-singer will have lost at least four pounds in weight and will need at least two days to recover.

A Sermon

There is a time when a performer, a member of the singing class, will consider his performance. What, he asks, has he achieved? He has worked, learned, discussed (sometimes), considered (sometimes) his brief. He has loved it, shaped it, mollified it (with fear) and has appeared at the end, heart in mouth but technique in place. He proceeds to the concert. He sings. It goes well, he feels. Yet what is the matter? The public won't join in, won't consider, are inert, dim, waiting to get home. So what has happened? On the other hand the opposite might well have been. If so, what has occurred?

A couple of years back I was elected (out of the blue) to an honorary fellowship of my old College – King's, Cambridge. It is the greatest honour that has been given to me. I know I have said that these things were of little worth, but I was comparing them with the highest of all accolades, the Love of God or, more nearly, ability in the Loving of God. There are very few honorary fellows extant at the *alma mater*. To be one is for me, who was particularly thick at academe – achieving, however, a small prize for creative writing and thence being called a 'Prizeman' – the joy of a prophet welcomed into his own country: a notoriously difficult feat. I was asked by the Dean (John Drury, a creative, imaginative and free theologian) whether I would be interested in writing and delivering a sermon. To this I agreed. It was to be about the spirit in performance. I arrived at a conclusion, or rather a speculation, which will be seen from the text. I, however, could not refrain from taking a swipe at those who believe that the art they see is more holy than it is, at those who out of fear will return time and again to one source of the spirit, little realising that the spring once drunk at will dry at the instant, and that the memory of easy slakings is all that is left. Anyway, no more of this; here is the text.

This short address was engendered by a conversation I had with the Dean. We were discussing the qualities of *The Dream of Gerontius* and our talk turned to the question of what makes some performances come to life or work and why others remain stubbornly inert, not to say dead. As I began later to consider this quizzler my thoughts led me to quite unexpected areas at which I hope to arrive.

If we consider the words 'come alive' or 'work' we must assume that these qualities are necessary to a performance. What is the 'life' and what is this 'working' that appear so essential to music or indeed any work of art?

As a performing artist, it is not generally required to use certain parts of the brain. The analytical bits (apart, of course, from the momentous debates of deciding whether Don Ottavio will for ever remain a wimp or whether one side of the stage or the other is more dramatic) are scrupulously shut away in a darkened upstairs room. However, when I consider the implication of this address – that is, the dissecting of the spirit – then this room must be opened and quickly.

Let us then assume that giving life to a performance implies giving spirit to the work. Here I go again. What is this spirit? I obviously must define this word, and with much trepidation will call it good or God or something ineffable but certainly a something in the mystical car. Therefore when a performance works it could be because I have invested it with a bit of God. This I feel is fair, but am now assuming that it must work only for me. This too is a valid position and one that I will return to. But for the moment let us consider that the perfect living, working performance must or should include all the players and all the audience. How can this be? What force is abroad when these criteria seem to be satisfied?

I recently went to rehearse a performance of *Gerontius*. It was an afternoon rehearsal for an evening show – not at all common these days. We were to do the piece with a chamber orchestra (admittedly a fine one, with the extra instruments added as necessary). The rehearsal was dire with these great musicians reading the dots, trying to make sense of them. The extremely notable contralto said something to the effect that the following performance would be like amateur night on the Blackpool Sands. The outcome was a miracle. Not simply because everyone for no apparent reason played themselves out of their skins, but also because the audience, for a similar unknown reason, gave of itself unstintingly – that the critics sought to see tulips where daffodils were growing I will ignore.

Another example. An unusual mélange of actors and singers, French and English text in a recent performance of *Béatrice et Bénédict* by Berlioz produced a spirit of such joy that it was almost tangible – that the critics saw pigs where springboks tangoed, I will ignore.

Such experiences are more common than one might think. The opposite is more likely, however. That *Mass in B Minor* in Lucca – the audience packed to the reliquaries – with a great conductor and a sumptuous cast limps into a half-remembered past. That possibly outstanding *Idomeneo* is chucked into forgetfulness.

For the mass joinings, I would like to advance an idea: this being that these weird unexpected blisses arrive because *one* lonely individual has suddenly found himself to be in touch with God. Eve in slow motion replaces the Golden Delicious. The separation in the garden has been reversed. This lonely one is now back home. He is close to the power and is sucked into a selfless bliss. A switch has been thrown, the lights are on. I mention that *one* has been taken; you then might ask why the sense of communal rapture.

Before I try and answer this, I must say that to watch this communal hysteria is not particularly edifying if you are not privy to the joy. I mention this because such happenings do occur when the performers are not particularly enamoured with the work. Usually with interpreters it is not a pre-requisite to like the piece. The notes are put in front of us and we perform them to the best of our ability, and for the composer and not specifically for the audience. (Of course I don't mean we – I mean me.) This opinion would be anathema for some musicians who can quite literally martyr themselves for *their* audience – as they call it. We can see examples of those who gave too much of themselves to the greedy public, been consumed and died. The adorers in their communal guilt then raise shrines to *their* dead – but this is by the way.

The Dream of Gerontius – which was so transcendental in its effect – is one of the great pieces that I am dubious about. I find the music remarkable in the honesty of its passion and commitment. At the same time I find it over-perfumed and redolent of a cringing posture and of self-indulgence. As to the poem of Newman I find the images dusty, the style quirky, the plot conventional, the theology, for my taste, infantile. I have spent some time trying to understand the 'mid-glory' and have concluded that it must be halfway to God. As my intuition tells me that at every second you are with God – should you choose to see it so – and that there is little more than the 'now' of God, naturally I find this thought perplexing.

There is worse to come. This example illustrates the obverse side of the mass transcendental reaction – showing that this need *not* only be of good origin. I sat and sang, or, more nearly, I sang and observed at a performance of *Caractacus* – again, I'm afraid, by Elgar. If Wagner had known nothing of voices he might have written it after a heavy night. I was singing in a weird, almost ridiculous, version of a bourgeois *Parsifal*. This difficult piece – *Caractacus,* that is – turned me into knots both physically and philosophically. I looked up, sweating profusely from the love-duet, and saw at least 40 per cent of the audience engaged in a titanic struggle to bite away the emotion. When Caractacus had sung to his dead comrades quite 60 per cent of contorted faces told of inner uncontrollable sobbings.

Caractacus is, by the way, a piece of unadulterated jingoism asserting – in the most inane libretto – that the fall of Rome was succeeded by the rise of glorious, all-healing Britain.

What I had witnessed was a Gloucestershire version of Hofbräuhaus meetings in Munich in the late thirties. This mass hysteria and sentimentality might be easily laughed off and put aside in the case of *Caractacus*, but from my crow's nest I see similar manifestations for the *B Minor Mass,* Mozart *Requiem* and *Missa Solemnis*. This is more discomforting.

To return to the point, I was enquiring why one person in his loneliness, and then with the sudden freedom that comes from the loss of the self, can influence three thousand people at a performance.

I ask you to consider the time when you – taking a short cut (and probably trespassing) – wandered into a field of sheep or cows. What happened? One animal spotted you, and in a tick the whole herd was watching you. Instant mass awareness in people is not unlike this. Our natural animal reaction is quickly accurate.

My temperament tells me that not only does man have a desperate need to rejoin God, but in his spiritual nakedness and isolation he also has a great desire for security. By the way, this need for security will naturally prevent him from the unity he desires, because as the self is preserved in security, the desired God is excluded. Nevertheless it is a powerful instinct, however misguided.

It is in this desire for security that I believe we explain the seeming passionate, unified bliss of thousands. As I have illustrated, this works irrespective of moral choice. Man finds security in packs and will seek this consolation in most areas whether they be political, artistic or religious.

Someone has been touched. The odour of touchment is abroad, others sniff it. So some performances become altars, so loneliness dies – at least until you get home.

I mentioned consolation and would like to follow this concept a little way. I would consider the reaction of the single soul who is responsible for the mass infection. He might even be a singer.

There is also a worm in *this* glorious bud. The ego gone, objectivity attained, the effect of the new unity is so great that tears pour from the eyes and immediately the self is re-established and restored. The intellect also being an immediate fellow, the reason for the rapture is analysed and sorted. If it is found to be, say, *Figaro* or a Van Gogh painting, then the piece will be revisited again and again in hope of the same reaction and result. The work of art has now become a consolation.

This word should not be used to imply a kind of mental infirmity or lack of spiritual backbone. However, my point is that over-familiarity with great art – and especially to the point when it becomes a comfort – will cause the same art to lose its purpose.

Does art, should art have a purpose, you might ask? I certainly believe so. I will say it again. Its purpose is to rid the listener and watcher of the ego – literally instantly and in the self-same instant to unify him with his Source. This instant occurs constantly, it keeps happening in equal validity from the cutting of a finger to the tasting of ice cream. If only our intellect would quit its muscling in with analysis and questionings, then we could be with our Ground more of the time.

The desire to return to the pleasure will eventually bar the same pleasure. Art becomes velvet shackles and the intellect the jailer that moves us further from the original moment of Satori with every backward glance. Art can preclude the development of the soul and can hold us like so many pieces of glazed fruit, good to consider and taste, but having lost the true tang of the now. Also every revisit takes precious seconds which might be better spent in open awareness of life as it skids by. Our need for security and desire for the social worker God bind our wings. Where we should fly, we hobble on scaly legs giving fearful praise and holding on.

I will conclude with a few sentences from Aldous Huxley: 'God isn't the son of memory. He's the Son of Immediate Experience. You can't worship a spirit in spirit unless you do it *now*. Wallowing in the past may be good literature. As wisdom it's hopeless. Time regained is paradise lost and Time lost is paradise regained. Let the dead bury their dead. If you want to live at every moment as it presents itself, you've got to die to every other moment.'

The Singer and Society

When I mentioned earlier that a singer is a commodity, I was stating an evident economic truth. He is also, equally evidently, a purveyor of a different truth, a verity more readily associated with the metaphysical or spiritual sides of man's nature. This intriguing dichotomy is also reflected in society. This in its time I believe can be very crudely divided into two temperaments – the first comprising citizens who ask only questions which are patently provable, and the second consisting of those who ask questions which have no logical or rational answer. The condition of a singer will be greatly influenced and altered depending on which of these temperaments is paramount in the government of the day.

It was recognised by the Greeks that a healthy society was judged by the equal representation of both these temperaments, that the negative should be balanced by the positive. I make no case for either in saying this – not yet, anyway.

As these temperaments are a fixed condition in the human psyche, it is not surprising that we find this struggle between pragmatism and intuition continuing through all human endeavour. Pragmatism I would link to a *posterior* knowledge, in other words knowledge which has been learned through experience and is capable of being proved by 'reason'. Intuition I would link to *a priori* knowledge – knowledge which is more concerned with those metaphysical or spiritual areas in which something is felt, or one is made aware of something. This second knowledge is unprovable, and therefore of little interest to those concerned with the first definition.

Even in the high-flown nit-picking world of philosophy there are clearly at least two schools. They might reasonably be called schools A and B. The first is concerned with academic philosophy, the second with a philosophy which is nearer theology and concerns itself with the said unprovable questions which naturally do not interest the students of A, who put aside such questions. Their chosen path takes them into what is for me the seriously sterile worlds of semantics, humanism and atheism. Naturally the B temperaments will find such 'ant-fucking' (as the Dutch so richly put it) infinitely tedious. B looks for that which can't be proved, and takes joy from it and comfort in it.

All democratically elected bodies will be comprised (more or less) of people with these two sorts of vision. I believe that, since most politicians are primarily interested in power and control, the majority of such elected assemblies will tend to be dominated by the pragmatic or A variety. The desire for such 'control' stems from an 'instancy' which is not only provable but malleable, and allows nothing for the possibility of 'outside' intervention which is in its nature uncontrollable.

I hear complaints at this. 'What about the religious fanatic?' I hear you say. 'What about ordered theocracy?' Your objections, I would answer, are perfect examples of political power masquerading in metaphysical vestments. The metaphysical/mystical impulse must be solitary. Banding together around it for any reason debases it and disfigures it into dimensions of political, ethnic groupings, a lonely soul comfort-taking.

As the first temperament is likely to dominate political expediency it is highly likely that the metaphysical argument will be given distinctly short shrift. Funds to aid the Magi of the arts will become extremely difficult to find, the money available being used for more practical and especially more conspicuous purposes. Bodies – highly visible – will be afforded care, while the soul – that different body within the body – will be ignored.

Under such extremely pragmatic conditions the life of the artist/ singer will become tough. Opportunities for showing the craft will be severely restricted; small but once flourishing music societies will be frozen from cash and will close. The government will be seen to be strong and handling the purse-strings with gloves of mail. It will be returned for further terms of power. The soul with the artistic impulse – always anarchistic if genuine – will likewise always be mistrusted by the more myopic practical soul. Not being understood, it will be made to look after itself. The question is heard: 'What society should need poetry – or any vision, come to that?'

I now (surprise, surprise), begin to betray my colours. The mystic

– being an anarchist, as asserted before, cannot be handled or categorised. He is, in today's political parlance, a loose cannon, a dangerous subverter of the given truth. He is therefore marginalised, even exorcised from the very society it is his born duty to feed. Note well what organised religions have done with the visionaries in their companies. Each has been cast out. Flaming intuition – straight from the source – always proves too dangerous, flying as it does so close to the dry tinder of religious/political orthodoxy. The heterodox has little solace in a society that demands stability for its existence.

And yet the artist-singer can never be ignored. Somewhere there are those who demand inner sustenance, who would be quite impoverished without the visionary impulse. Even the power-hungry notice an echo in its soul. Something is missing. The politician, well read (sometimes), urbane, will divine that the missing ingredient is that thing which his anarchic opponents are constantly harping about. He is clever (sometimes) and beefs up his understanding of the opus numbers, of an outré composer – let's call him Dick Persempre – and in so doing he will be seen by his superiors as a possible Arts Minister. He will still be the man that never knew love.

The need for the magus, the shaman, the art priest is seeded deep in archetypical man. This need must be catered for, or he will go mad. The future for the artist is always gold with promise, the present always fraught with prickly brakes and dangers. This is immutable law. The singer is the smallest of small cogs in the wheel which turns the constant discussion of pro or contra the soul of man with its limitations and possibilities.

With a little careful observation, a pleasing irony can be noted. Those who are magisterial mandarins of pragmatism while in office often suffer a quick but substantial sea change when out of the same. The old 'metaphysically dispossesed' begin almost miraculously to appear on all manner of artistic advisory boards. All the great art institutions of Britain are in the hands of such people. Many of these appointments are in the gift of the Cabinet. It is as if they're being thanked for their *serious* work by being given a spiritual toy to play with as they embrace their senility. So an artist – like me – can take comfort and chuckle, with ever so gentle malice, as I see Sir Flatulent Fart beginning his apotheosis and sharp ascension to a *de facto* priest. Those once looked on with such humorous disdain are now the body of society; those insolent, not too intelligent artists are now the blood of the people. The parvenus then begin to make 'artistic' decisions which can affect my life. They have forgotten that I am the purveyor of a certain truth. So they arrive at the plateau of high art. They are now 'political priests', and a more untrustworthy combination I cannot conceive.

Simply watch all this, young singer. It is an eternal process which will not change – not even when professionals achieve high artistic office.

Don Basilio

There often comes a time when a well-known singer will be asked to take on a small part. I must hasten to add that, when on stage in the heat of the battle, there is no such thing. A small part might be more accurately defined as a minor character in the drama. Having already expressed my ideas on performing two of the so-called leading roles, I now feel it could be illuminating to analyse the quality of thought which might invest a small part with fresh interest and, at the same time, probably alter the usual balance of the opera. I shall therefore consider the character of Don Basilio from *Le Nozze di Figaro* of Mozart. How can I make his character mine? The condition of a singer hangs on such philosophical idiocies.

What kind of man is Basilio? First, I think it's probably easier to decide what he is not. To do this I must consider the way he is usually played. There is a tradition, probably from Mozart's own time, of Basilio being played as a crude, heavily comic 'character'. The word 'character' here implies an unusual walking style (often slightly stooped and he might even be limping with hands pressed sanctimoniously together), an unusual make-up (to this very day some of the older hands play him with a false nose) and a voice which is meant to match the general seediness of the character (usually effected by whining unpleasantly through the nose). The fact that he must sing a beautiful aria seems to be ignored. Thousands of Basilii have squawked their way through the part, or so long-tongued history will have it. I have my doubts on the veracity of historical tradition and feel no compulsion to follow too closely the steps of my predecessors. I must realise that I am unique, and act accordingly. I have been forced to watch masterpieces of art being mutilated in their cleaning – no concessions here to the inexorable workings of time. I have been compelled to hear performances of authentic music with no trace of humanity. I will now do my bit for authenticity and be myself.

Basilio is a man of great intelligence. He is, I believe, more intelligent than anyone else in the Almaviva household. He is a musician, a priest, a thinker, a gossip. If I analyse these attributes it becomes clear that he must be a man of sensitivity and subtlety – already the stereotypes are beginning to fall. It is true that there are many time-servers in the Church, the conservatoire and academe, and that Basilio could be one of this persuasion. I choose the other option, for in so doing the character becomes more deep, more interesting.

In the house he is ubiquitous – his eyes are everywhere, his nose constantly sniffing the wind. I think it is most important for the establishment of the character that he is observed watching the passing of the canzonetta from Cherubino to Susanna. This immediately establishes his power, his danger. There must be no sign of the cretinous buffoon here.

However, we cannot get very far into the character of Don Basilio without looking in detail at his fourth Act aria. Some think it unfortunate that Mozart put this important aria at the end of the opera. They do have one point – at this juncture of a long opera, the audience is tiring and might wish to go home or to dinner. If the aria is cut, which is sometimes the case, the character of Don Basilio becomes extremely hard to play simply because the chance of explaining his character to the audience has been taken away, all the earlier behaviour seeming merely eccentric or stupid. Mozart knew exactly what he was doing when he placed that aria in the last Act. He wished to make a point concerning the musician/thinker's position in a philistine aristocratic house of the period. Don Basilio's frustrations, impotence and solution probably mirror Mozart's own house closely. The aria 'In quelli anni cui dal poco' is his credo. In it he explains his philosophy and shows how it has helped him to survive – more or less untouched – the fooleries of class and politics that have always surrounded him.

Basilio calmly but firmly announces a rather Zen-like idea: in order to survive one should never confront things head on but should rather side-step them, let them pass impotently by, losing force as they go. One should confuse others with malleable behaviour and non-convergent logic.

So Basilio arrives, perhaps nicely oiled, with Bartolo in a sweet-smelling Spanish garden at night. He senses a truth, a reality that sustains him through those endless servile hours. He is relaxed, he can be himself. He is in the presence of Fate, of his mentor Lady Fortune (Donna Flemma). Almost as at Confession, he starts to spill the story of his life. Whether Bartolo understands or in fact even listens is of little importance.

I must say in passing that I would love to have read Don Basilio's memoirs, had he written any (perhaps one of his kind did, and they have been lost and are waiting to be discovered). The razor tongue, the beady cold eye could have told us so much of the social history of the time. In fact, in my belief the memoirs of any of the characters in the opera would have been interesting with the possible exception of the Count and Figaro, both of whom I find monumentally tedious. And Barbarina doesn't hold too many interests, unless of course one considers her fantasies – but that would be another kind of book. No, *The Stiletto of Seville* would have made the most marvellous social history, full of truthful bias.

They are in the garden when Figaro enters. 'What are you doing here?' he says. Basilio replies, 'You asked us to come, so here we are.' Figaro rants jealously on and leaves. Basilio replies that Figaro seems to have the devil in him simply because the Count is meeting Susanna late at night in the garden. He continues that he doesn't understand why Figaro should be so upset. After all, he says, this is no unusual, remarkable situation – it is so commonplace as to be boring; and anyway, should Figaro object, what could he possibly gain? This is part of Basilio's philosophy. He is convinced that man's nature is unchangeable, and we should not be surprised if we find part of his nature unacceptable. If we seek happiness we must be happy to start off with, because it is not findable. One can accuse Basilio of being uninvolved with the blood and guts of life. We must not, however, forget that he is a remarkably clever and intelligent man who sees the problems – those which vex others – from a further dimension. Understanding and love will only proceed if you view life from an eternal dimension. (Basilio says that once, a long time ago, when he was young he too yearned for power and thought he could influence the world – don't forget he was and is a musician and man of the spirit. His early passions were soon knocked out of him and he suddenly realised, with the help of Donna Flemma (not the spirit of God, notice), that he had been behaving in the most stupid of ways. She advised him to wear the ass's skin (*penne di somaro*) in order to be and play the fool, and in so doing confuse the aggressor. Of course there is a price to pay for such action, and that is the loss of the self, the ego. Basilio follows his karma and notices that, with the loss of his desire and arrogance, he can see much further. He attains a certain wisdom and he sees others' foolishness. Basilio is the piece of flotsam cast up on the eternal beach; the others float aimlessly for ever.

At this point I was about to write quite comprehensively about the role of the pre-pubescent boy in the works of Benjamin Britten. Humphrey Carpenter has beaten me to it and I am mightily relieved. He has gone about the task with a tact and scrupulous attention to detail that it is not in my nature to achieve. One thing, however, remains. I have to add, rather waspishly, that no one has yet counted the numbers of times the whip is used in Britten's works. There must be a PhD for someone here.

Artificial Music

I beg singers to beware of the record companies. They are like a great company spider. They will seduce you, mate with you, and then consume you and keep your shoes for someone else. I do not wish to under-estimate the contribution that the companies have made to the dissemination of the musical gospel. To Radio 3 and records we owe the growth – to gigantic proportions – of an art form once considered elitist. (That some still use this epithet when talking betrays them as political time-servers and not artists.) Record companies do make enormous profits as they spread the gospel, but that fact should not diminish the achievement. My concern rests on their methods of money-making, my warning is intended to soften the blow of future disappointments.

To keep the tills ringing, the companies must sell records. Because we live in a ludicrous economic system that believes growth is the universal panacea (never visualising the final outcome of this philosophy) without which civilised society would collapse, they must sell more and more records. How do they do this?

They begin by looking at the musical literature and the various sales, noting that only certain composers and periods are bought by enough people. Mozart, Beethoven, Bach and Wagner all sell. They now notice with some consternation that they have recorded all the best-selling pieces many times. What can be done? The answer is simplicity itself. Why, record them all again in a different way. Better than this even! Why not also change the methods of reproduction? Change the systems again and again. Now everything will have to be bought new, and at the same time the competition might be put out of business. This has happened four times in my experience: 78 and 33^1/$_3$ revolutions, 12 inch and 7 inch discs were quickly followed by cassettes, lasers and CDs. There is more to come: the system is set up and right for tinkering.

The music too was reinvented. 'How can you reinvent music?' I hear you cry. Well, it's simple really. The gullible public cannot be guaranteed to buy Karajan's tenth version of Beethoven's Fifth. It well may show the maestro's ageing maturity, a new philosophical insight, a new speed perhaps – perhaps even a favouring of the horns, yet the music remains stubbornly and distressingly the same. (I notice that each 'new' conductor as he appears believes that he has his own version of the 'Choral' Symphony. The symphony, however, remains unmoved.) He may favour a slight rubato in the oboe; it sounds much as it did. The violins, apart from the odd changed bowing, are disquietingly similar. The last movement of the Jupiter Symphony of Mozart might be much quicker, but the structure doesn't bend. The companies realise this and decide it is essential that the whole perspective of these great classic pieces must be changed. What, then, can be done?

In an obscure concert, in an equally obscure hall, an academic musician – by academic I mean one who has more gift for analysis and discussion than for performing – is trying an experiment. He has recently read a thesis, long lost, on the performing style of the eighteenth century. He reads and inwardly digests.

Guido Hand is discussing his new theory with a friend. They are drinking instant coffee from not very well washed mugs in an elegant but messy room in an institute of academe. The air is heavy with many promises. The conversation proceeds.

G.H.: 'You know what, luvvie? I really think we're on to something!'
Friend: 'Exciting, isn't it, sweetie?'
G.H.: 'Sure is.'
Friend: 'What is, sweetie?'
G.H.: 'I've felt for some time now that music, especially eighteenth-century gear needed a face-lift. You know what I mean?'
Friend: 'Not really, duckie.'
G.H.: 'Well, I think it needs to have all that make-up taken off. Get back to the skin. See what's there.'
Friend: 'Sounds a bit drastic to me. How would you do it?'
The academic pauses, pregnant with thought, rises, goes to the kettle, refills it and throws the switch.

G.H.: 'More coffee?'

Friend: 'No thanks, I'm not getting enough sleep as it is.'

G.H.: 'I think I will. With this idea I'm not going to sleep anyway.'

Friend: 'Well, go on. What are you going to do?'

The academic slowly lowers himself on to a greasy black leather sofa and continues.

G.H.: 'First let's think what's wrong. At the moment the strings are too dominant, yet strangely indistinct, too well fed, too comfortable – in a word too professional. The wind is android and basically lost in string sound. The horns are too secure and – oh yeh! – the percussion is too woolly. It's bloody dull.'

Friend: 'I do know what you mean, luv, I listened to a performance of *Figaro* at Salzburg last year when the orchestra – although it was really interested in the stage and though it sported really individual sound especially the woodwind – sounded as if it was playing the score from an underground bunker (no offence intended) [*here he tittered*] and was perfectly boring – and I use both words judiciously.'

G.H.: 'Then you do know what I mean. Let's consider the bow. The old one was arched, you know, hence the name. [*The word 'hence', suddenly changed the tone. Now it became serious.*] As it is of this shape, then it must lose intensity as it is drawn across the strings.'

The friend has not noticed the conversation's gravitational change.

Friend: 'OK, sweetie, with you, go on.'

G.H. is slightly discomfited.

G.H.: 'Therefore, stupid, as the phrase continues it gets weaker.'

Friend: 'Now I'm not sort of with you, luvvie. Tell me why.'

G.H.: 'No *why* here, Babs [*he sometimes called him Babs*]. I've invented acceptable modern music. I'm on to something huge. Listen! Let's consider the wind [*he notices his friend's unspoken quip and silences him with a look*]. No, let's consider violin style. Why do they vibrate all the time? The answer – you don't know, do you?'

Friend: 'Yes, I do, smartie-drawers. They do it to keep in tune to keep a mean pitch. Therefore if two are playing slightly sour of each other, a gentle vibration will bring them more nearly into tune. I read acoustics too, remember. Listen duckie, when I was in Salzburg I

heard a Hungarian folk band. They played in the street sounding
obstinately rough, looking unanimously dowdy and sending forth
miraculous energetic power. The fiddler trilled on every note. Why?
Now it's my turn to ask and answer. His technique allowed him no
singing bel canto legato. There is, you know, a misapprehension that
bel canto is of eighteenth-century origin. It is in fact far older and
is founded in the breath control of the Muslim muezzin. [*Slightly
embarrassed at this fount full of knowledge he takes a break, shrugs
his shoulders and says disarmingly:*] Trill, shrill, legato, shribrato –
who cares as long as they love their music?'

G.H.: 'You've got it, buggerlugs, clever old sod! We'll stop them
from vibrating. Keep the left hand steady, make them sweat. Not
only sweat, but leave them feeling embarrassed when they play to
the end of a note. I've got it. This will be the "dying fall" new
music.'

Friend: 'Brilliant, you clever swine, you bonny-boots.'

G.H.: 'Oh! make up your mind.'

Friend: 'Which do you prefer?'

G.H.: 'Bonny-boots.'

Friend: 'OK, bonny-boots, how are you going to find musicians
to play like this?'

G.H.: 'I've already thought of that. I will look to the universities,
the cradles of the thinking classes. In those stones lurk fine talent,
but talent which is embarrassed by professionalism. The good try
that fails is their ultimate goal. The talent is enormous – convince
them that "professional" is not a dirty word, and we have a
revolution.'

Friend: 'The wind? The brass?'

G.H.: 'Although it's alien to the true breaking style, they will
follow the strings – after all, there are more of them. They'll come
on board, absolutely no problem.'

Friend: 'You'll need choirs. What about them?'

G.H.: 'Same answer. Grab the most intelligent voices from
ecclesiastical choirs – add some clever girls [*remember, most of
these souls saw themselves condemned to the lives of teachers or
city brokers*]. I'll get rid of their ridiculous consonants and mould
them into a virtuoso unit.'

Friend: 'Don't you think you ought to find the correct nationality
to sing this "new music" – after all, the singers from England

are hardly like Italian singers and probably never were. The temperaments are so different.'
Here he is interrupted imperiously.
G.H.: 'No, no. No time for that.

And so it happened. At that inauspicious concert, in that remarkably inauspicious concert hall, a style was formed that would reinvent music for a while. It was called 'authentic'. Such it could never have been. It might have been called 'new', for that certainly it was. That it gave the record companies resurrection cannot be doubted.

The public wouldn't notice that passionate Italian music was being sung by timorous callow Anglicans. They wouldn't be interested. They wouldn't listen to the English accents, they'd be inspired by the new sharp defined sound. Don't forget it would also be their own sound, for the paying public were but a generation on. They would adore the pyrotechnics, they would think that this too is the sound of the past.

Having written this silly satire I was most encouraged to note that real academics are now proving the lie of authenticity. Robert Philip, in his book *Early Recordings and Musical Style*, supports my point well – if, however, in a far more intelligent, ordered way.

The King Is Dead . . .

I was, if I remember correctly, attempting to warn the following generation of singers of the power of the market, which in its most gross manifestation is shown in the dealings of the record companies. This year at Salzburg (and never forget that the Salzburg Festival is one that was hi-jacked by and for the record companies) I was pleasantly surprised with the change of scene. I don't, of course, refer to the magnificent mountains which surround the city and look for all eternity like the teeth in God's bottom jaw. Nor do I refer to the *Ausarbeiter* who collect horse shit and are called (imaginatively, I thought) *Rossknödelsammler*; neither to those inexplicably intense feelings that when I walk the Judengasse I should do so goose-stepping and with my right hand raised high. Rather, I refer to the advertisements. The town is covered with faces. Walls stuck with faces, sweet shops candied with faces. Small faces, large ones, winsome ones, Dutch ones, retiring ones, stupid ones, possibly intelligent ones stalk you as you walk through this architectural masterpiece. The general impression of these heads – and I suppose one shouldn't be surprised at the Celtic influence (head hunters to a man), so close is it to Hallstatt – is one of surprised stupidity, as if the possessor had been goosed by God and would not be changed by it. Arrogance, insolence, innocence, vacancy all are covered on those weeping boards. Each is, however, being flattered by its record company, each massaged in an area of erotic egoism that it has not dreamed of in its wildest extravaganza. We cannot die, comes the message. Because we are here, we live. So beautiful, so sad, rebounds the echo; so talented, so myopic, comes another. I'm rich but liberated, says one. I may be dumb but I'm powerful, says the next. Oh, what a mess!

My point is that six years ago all the faces were different. But I must define myself more clearly: all the lungs and fingers presently earning the company money were different. The singers, pianists and violinists previously but no longer given top billing have not suddenly become worst artists – with the passage of time and with their growing experience they should have become finer performers – and no new faces are needed to sell new records. All the oldest of lags were there, at least those still alive – a kind of living *Denkmal*: no longer capable of doing a proper job, but a reminder to the public that the companies have some loyalty, appreciate service to the great god Croesus (the companies must, after all, convince the public that they are interested in art). These oldest living artists are a cemetery of early money and wear the tarnished badges of long service.

All the real earners had, however, been changed: the old replaced by new birds, all in fresh plumage, all tweeting and strumming as if none had done so before. To be honest, life has always been so; long before the advent of the gramophone people were superseded, pensioned off. My point is that the star of today and especially the *étoile* of tomorrow must beware. As an aside, I notice that there was no sign of Karajan. The fact that God is so easily replaced is, I feel, a comment on the genesis of God. I shall leave it at that.

Musical PC

The time has come for a little humour. I use both words with studied
discretion. Humour, mostly in the forms of jokes or anecdotes, plays
an important role in the lives of most musicians and singers. This
is, I believe, because the moment of laughter is perhaps even more
complete than that of sexual release. 'How long is eternity?' said
the aspirant. 'Just long enough for a laugh,' answered the sage. I
know I've mentioned this before, but its relevance is even greater
when used in reference to the high-wire tension of performing. The
grand, gross guffaw defeats the coming uncertainties of the show,
the riotous anecdote laughs in the face of fearsome fate.

Most musical jokes are related to a perceived under-class of
performer. The viola, for example, has a lexicon all to itself far
more than the solos it's required to play. From the clichéd stupider
singing – tenor and soprano – sprout remarkable goodies.

Luckily, music is a particularly non-political area. (When did you
last see a student revolt at any of the great musical seats of learning?)
So such jokes are accepted and laughed at with kind relish. The viola
jokes are, of course, Polish jokes or Irish ones or dwarf jokes or bald
jokes, or in fact any related to the dear condition of man. Nannying
political correctness has tried to put a stop to such things. It has
invaded the dictionary as a postulant raids the holy grail, in hope
of change through words and attitude, little realising that the fact
that you might call me, for example, 'follicularly disadvantaged'
does nothing to change my hairless condition. Whatever you call
me, I remain as stubbornly bald as Byron remained stubbornly
club-footed. I wish to return to political correctness later, in yet
another onslaught on authentic music. But for now enough of the
polemic and on to the jokes.

A neatly bitchy one was current quite recently. It concerns the
modern – authentic – interpretation of Mozart conductors. It would,

I think, be rather invidious of me to include my own hated list – just look at that commended by the critics for modern praise, and reverse it. I leave you, therefore, to provide your own list. Three or four major conductors are travelling in the same car (this is a joke in itself when I remember their general mutual hostility). They are following a mountain road. Each turn gets tighter and more frightening. Suddenly the car goes out of control and hurtles with its load four thousand feet to its and their destruction. 'Who was saved?' comes the line. The answer: 'Mozart.' Supply your own names and you'll get acres of laughter off this one.

Here are three more conductor jokes (I'll then move on). 'What is the difference between Scholl's sandals and a conductor?' Answer: 'The sandals buck up the feet.' The second: 'Why is a conductor like a condom?' 'It's safer with but better without.' Third: 'What is the ideal weight of a conductor?' 'Twelve ounces plus the urn.'

So on to the viola jokes. 'How do you make a viola play vibrato?' Answer: 'You write "solo" above the part.' 'What is the fourth and most testing examination for the viola?' 'Opening the case from memory.' And this. A viola player has serious psychological problems. He decides he must go to a psychiatrist. He puts on his best suit and a rather fine fedora hat. The receptionist says that Dr Sinopoli is ready. He walks in, sits down and takes his hat off. Dr Sin says, 'I've never seen anything like it. How long have you had that on your head?' The frog answers, 'Oh! It started as a boil on my bum.'

Tenor jokes – just one, naturally and niggardly. 'What is the difference between a *leggero* tenor (*tenorino*), a lyric tenor and a Heldentenor.' 'The first has no balls, the second one, the third two and he's standing on both of them.' Finally the best soprano joke. 'How do you tell the difference between a Wagnerian soprano and a pit bull terrier?' Answer: 'The jewellery.'

That's the sort of thing. In these scherzi it is possible to define a warmth, a natural state of things, that speaks of regard, of amicability, of dear acceptance. I fear the time when the edict forbids viola jokes, tenor, size, race or intellect jokes, when every neonate viola must be spared this joy, this truth and must play sterile and impotent in life's broken consort. To be whole they must learn to deflect the arrows of fortune, not hope that the *flèches* will be outlawed and consigned to giants' toothpicks. I offend again: I presume that the food giants eat warrants toothpicks, also that arrows are far too big in their nature – oh dear!

The environment of music has to be one of competition, or standards can only reach the mediocre. This, you may feel, is fine in that one burst of excellence is not worth the humiliation of even one soul; and you may well have a point. But to protect the ungifted in one area from a true vision of themselves precludes their possibility of growth, of finding what is indeed their unique gift. Every person is in some way an original. So to cosset falsely is an act of patronisation and equally of self-aggrandisement, a need for control hiding in the coloured coat of care. If such an attitude became the norm we would need to play cricket without stumps, bat or ball, football with no posts and golf without clubs, and to go swimming without water. The idea is, of course, madness and shows that its source springs from an impotence that I shall discuss in my final assault on that winsome figment known as 'authentic' music.

There is a thought in the more intellectual circles (or at least there has been until recently) that it is possible, even desirable, to perform or represent a work of art without the preferences and genes of the self being represented – a desire to represent the text without personal involvement. This is the belief of a somewhat dated French idea called post-structuralism. Les Messieurs Foucault and Derrida believe that the solipsistic 'I' of every imagining, every dream, every action, every word is an illusion – all that might be relied upon was and is the text. They see the writer as the 'author function', and might see the musical creator the 'composer function'.

I'm probably wrong, of course, but my vision of working with Pierre Boulez in the mid-seventies on many projects, but most notably the reconstruction and performance of the first complete *Lulu*, is of a person desperately but failingly trying to get his enormous personality out of the way. When he conducted Haydn he endeavoured to show structure, sound and the like, but never to interpret the feelings he might have suspected were either his or the composer's.

This decision was not, I felt, a musical nor particularly a philosophical one, but rather a political gesture. No, that's not quite accurate. It was a philosophical political gesture. It arose from a fundamental misreading of man's nature by the liberal intelligentsia (of which he was a high-ranking commander). I am indebted to

Robert Hughes in his book *The Culture of Complaint* for some of the following political ideas. As he did not follow his critique into the forest of musical taste, however, and I saw an irresistible connection, I hope that he will forgive me.

In the late nineteenth century there were two colossi who clubbed the world with their misguided annoyance. Wagner was one. He thought himself a high intellectual. He was in fact a magician, a demagogic cult leader preaching a version of genetic purity that was still being echoed in Eliot about a century later, and is now heard in the fearsome babblings of 'born again Christians'. Around him assembled those dispossessed of confidence, of love, of thought, those who needed a leader with all the answers whose word was law. This was the character later and more virulently echoed in Junes and Howell, those cult leaders (I hear strange Welsh Protestant reverberations in the names) who led their glad followers to death in Guyana and Waco. If Christ were ever to reappear, his fate would be the same – as, of course, it was in his time. Wagner is all magical toxicity and wrong.

The second of these controllers was Karl Marx. He made two fatal mistakes. The first was in not believing the genetic greed of the mass of mankind, the second in not believing the fearfulness of the lonely soul of man. It takes an honest man to accept his loneliness in the face of all; to realise his inability to communicate exactly with another of his species (especially through the word); to accept that at birth we are alone and also at death. Marx wrongly assumed that in this loneliness man would group around class and inequality. He didn't. He grouped instead around family and race. He believed Les Valseurs in the loincloth rather than that rational thinker in the head. The intellectuals believed Marx. The collapse of Marxism proved them wrong. These would be no class alignment. Instead man went to home ground, to fighting and wars, to the haven of ethnic security.

Capitalism having won the field with no casualties, where was there left to go? The answer was into issues, into psychology, into care and above all into art. In this last was an area of possible power where the hurt of lost illusions might find the balm of legitimacy. So the disadvantaged, both culturally and politically, were to be 'cared' for. How was that to be done? By minimising the previous gods, who could not promote this new vision of political correctness. Out of such thinking sprang many of the teachers of the humanities of recent times. 'Authentic' music is from this same branch. It is a cousin of the defeated 'now' which was so important to the intellectual process of the last twenty-five years.

Its insistence on text and sound is the spawn of Derrida and Foucault, or at least of the *Zeitgeist* which spawned them. I have no argument with the uniqueness of the soul and the unique utterance of the same. My problem occurs when things of ancient and proven spiritual worth are debased in order not to make another soul seem second-rate or a failure. The culture of man is a bowl of minestrone soup which becomes richer with every addition. If we choose to separate and isolate, then the soup will become water and the various entities in its construction bland, uninteresting in their repetition. The ingredients are – of course – distinct cultures and souls. Political correctness would wish to prevent the mix lest one ingredient was thought inferior. Such is the problem with 'authentic' music. Here we are led to believe that the text has been misinterpreted through the action of romanticism and time, that somehow the ideal has been corrupted as it has passed through the hands of the raping individual of time. It must be put back to be rediscovered, saved and worshipped. The text is there, is absolute (unlike those of any of the early poets such as Homer and Plato, who have been passed down to us by that now despised race, the Arabs). So the text is there in its daring fecundity. Unfortunately with music, one does need sound to activate it. What, then, would be the politically correct action? Why, to ban the instruments of paternal romanticism, of course, and to replace them with theory – a theory in which even the minimally gifted could pick up an instrument and express themselves. (Each blessed individual therefore has something unique to say.) As I said before, I have no argument with the necessity of love, but it does stop when the genuine poet is castrated on the altar of the spurious god 'Carewareness' (now there's a good new word for the Oxford Dictionary).

The text of sound has therefore been invented on politically correct lines. So the great Romantic Bach's images of blood (a musical Rubens if ever there was one), pain and grief are shown until they appear as introverted as the works of Egon Schiele. The grand, singing lines of Mozart symphonies are chopped and fall to pieces. The sequences in which the voice should sing into the tie, thereby creating exquisite discord, are mainly ignored as an embarrassment, and masquerading as style and tact. The final effect is, however, not one of minutely observed clarity of text. Just as Boulez could not perform Haydn without his distinct intellectual wry humour showing through, our authentic men attempt to re-create the classic master pieces. The outcomes are personal, often judgemental readings of Olympian authoritarianism and frigidity. This I don't resent in any way. It merely goes to prove my point that solipsism will finally out. There is no way of escaping the personal thumbprint. Any performer who seeks to discover and then perform original text is ingenuous. The intellect – which has always tried to divorce itself from its container, the body – is imprisoned. It is the captive of pitiless nature and nurture, in that order. Nevertheless, although Bach, Mozart or virtually any eighteenth-century composer cannot be understood by us as by their contemporaries, we can still be illumined with their imaginative possibilities. There is not a cultural memory as such – no archetypical well in which we may lower our empty buckets and, in drawing them up, find truth; at least not one which we may rely upon, share or defend in argument. This is where Derrida is right and the art of the critic is useless. He is wrong in being too specific, too measurable, too short in time, too needful of control, too myopic of eternal dimension.

'Authentic' music has been a nostalgic cultural development, one of the reasons, as explained earlier, being the exclusion of the left from political power, another the fear for the dying self and the need to fill the space of that dying soul with objects of its own culture. I use the words 'has been' because I firmly believe that such a nostalgic movement is already showing distinct signs of ossification. I can see the modern taste being viewed in a hundred years' time as only a product of its time – a time of no confidence and distinct fear for the future. The record-ings will be regarded rather as we look on dinosaur finds, as interesting but not essential to the development of the soul of man.

The major surprise is that this modern-old music has been swallowed so wholly by the critical establishment. There has been virtually no voice raised, even in question. They have fallen meekly into the plans – the fiscal plans of the record companies. When, however, I look at the class and education of most of the critics

I should not be surprised, for they are mostly of that politically deracinated elite about whom I have been speaking.

Not long ago, Hilly (my wife) and I were visiting a friend of ours who is currently going through the severe pain of divorce. (Her husband was evidently too suspect to the 'chemistry' of another. It could of course be called 'lust'. This is another example of the duplicity of words. Words do not alter the nature of anything. If one called a giraffe a cloud it would never alter the essence of the animal, and vice versa.) Once she had told us the rights and wrongs, dabbed her eyes a little and given us some food, she asked us whether we would like to listen to some music. Normally I would say no, but the situation seemed to demand music. She knew that I had been singing *The Magic Flute* in Spain – more of that later – so thoughtfully she chose a CD and played it. The recording was of the same piece, but the performance was one of such quality that it took my breath away. Klemperer had made it in the early sixties. Through the haze of memory I remembered being a member of the chorus. Nicolai Gedda – the best tenor of my times – Lucia Popp, Gottlob Frick, Gundula Janowitz, Gerhard Unger, all were in finest form. It was, however, the conducting that was so remarkable. The performances in Madrid had been ordinary in the extreme, and here I heard the piece in all its magic and mystery. The speeds were inevitable, the love and care palpable. I thought of our modern performances, all theory, all textual, with no concern for the spirit of the Earth so centred in Mozart's vision. Instead of real understanding – and by that I mean a vision of philosophic unity from the eternal dimension – we are served technical brilliance, muscular vapidity and spiritual ignorance.

Klemperer

Having mentioned the genius of Klemperer, I feel I should tell of my first dealing with him. I was a fresh young tenor in the Ambrosian Chorus, the only truly freelance professional chorus that London has ever boasted. We were preparing to sing the *Missa Solemnis* – that informed masterpiece of granite – with the Philharmonia Orchestra conducted by the great Otto. I moseyed along to Gandhi Hall, somewhere near Tottenham Court Road, and picked up my score. I had never seen nor heard the work before. You must remember that the choir of King's College, Cambridge was not nearly so catholic in taste as it is now, and also there was a definite bias against Beethoven in the early sixties (too authoritarian, I suppose). We were set up in our vocal phalanxes awaiting the great man. He arrived and announced in clear English – his stroke, and with it his imitatable speech defect, came later – that the soloists had not arrived. Schwarzkopf was the soprano. Ernst Haefliger was the tenor, Agnes Giebel was the alt, and the bass is now lost in time as they have a habit of doing, being too cumbersome for its fleet motion. J. McCarthy, the chorus fixer, was called. Could he produce a quartet to fill in? He could, he did and I found myself at about twenty-three sight-reading the *Missa* to Klemperer. I cannot forget the experience. He spent the whole time teaching us the work. He did it with courtesy and patience. I have since sung it many, many times, regarding it as one of the works which could have been written for my voice. The experience with Klemperer was seminal.

I recall singing in the same choir a few years later, this time in the famous Methodist Kingsway Hall which was used frequently by EMI for its recordings – it had a perfect natural reverberance which is, sadly, almost impossible to find in any of the modern halls. The chorus master of the Philharmonia Chorus at this time was a nice rubicund Austrian called Wilhelm Pitz. He was Klemperer's right hand – the conductor had just had the stroke which left him partially paralysed and bereft of energy except perhaps for small intense bursts. Klemperer used now to sit to conduct, while Pitz stood behind moving his arms and conducting like a dervish. (I must mention, simply for accuracy, that the Ambrosian Chorus often 'stiffened' this amateur chorus. Not a pleasant verb, I find, but accurate.)

The recording was of the *B Minor Mass*. I have no idea who the soloists were – anyway, on that session we were singing only the choruses. The first hour and twenty minutes had gone well. We took a break and returned to do one of the quietest sections of the mass. Singing gently away, we noticed that Klemperer was dropping off. His stick was in his hand and we thought it would fall, ruining what was rather a good take. Pitz kept beating behind the podium; the conductor finally fell asleep, didn't drop his stick, and that section was completed without him ever knowing it.

The next two Klemperer stories concern the baritone Dietrich Fischer-Dieskau. Klemperer was never one for new-fangled styles – so when the Watkins Shaw edition of the *Messiah* was published with the recent scholarship, showing that the singers should sing lengthy cadenzas, he was not impressed. In one of his cadenzas Dieskau went into orbit, singing through all the notes and most of the keys he was capable of. When he returned to the tonic, Klemperer said through the left side of his mouth: 'Welcome home, Herr Fischer.' Note the diminution of his name here, done no doubt to keep this star singer well in his place. About this time Dieskau began to conduct. (Yes, even baritones try it; it's not always the tenors.) As he was singing for Klemperer at the time he went up to the maestro and told him that he would be conducting Schubert's *Unfinished Symphony* with the Philharmonia the following week. He said, 'Dr Klemperer, I will be conducting Schubert at the Royal Festival Hall, it would be very kind if you could find the time to come.'

Klemperer answered wittily, 'Certainly, Herr Fischer, but only if you come to my recital of the *Winterreise*.'

He was a wicked old goat, too. I remember him chasing an extremely well-known English alto – of not too great a sense of humour, but some holiness – around Edinburgh shouting: '*Ich muss ein Weib haben!*' (I must have a woman).

In those far-off days Klemperer was thought to conduct all music very slowly. But if you listen you can see this is far from the truth. The impression of slowness was in fact an awareness of space and time. He let everything speak. He was one of those great old maestri who, having great self-confidence, didn't feel the necessity to make macho gestures whether in speeds or ego. I suppose it was a slower world then, and if music – or at least its interpretation – is governed by the *Zeitgeist*, then it should be slower. However, where does that leave our interpretations of old music? Since it took days and days to travel from Linz to Paris in the eighteenth century, why do we rush through Mozart's music at such a suicidal pace? They spent hours at their concerts and hours at their meals. Our concentration lasts just about as long as it takes the advertisements to break up a programme on TV. We graze, we eat on the hoof. We fly to New York from London in three hours. Should the speed of our living not warn us? Should we not be careful in visiting this hectic vision on a slower, different age? Should we not – if we are interested in authenticity – measure our allegro against theirs? Metronome markings are dubious. Beethoven once sent a symphony to the Royal Philharmonic Society in London and followed it on request with metronome marks. These were later lost, so the Society asked for more. Beethoven sent them. Meanwhile, the original paper was found. They were markedly different. It is impossible for us to live in another time, to know and feel as they did. To be aware of this is at least a beginning to better understanding.

The Diary

Singers find themselves chasing their trade all over the world, and bemoan the fact. A successful international singer will, if he is lucky, spend seven months of each year at home. The rest, those remaining seemingly empty five months away from home, must be filled. How they are occupied depends entirely on the temperament of the individual. Some shop obsessively, some eat manically, others indulge other appetites. I generally fill my time with reading. The books I care for are mostly of the philosophical mystical branch of literature. I do, however, enjoy reading and rereading the classic books of the canon. I have recently read three translations of the *Divine Comedy*, a book on Meister Eckhart the mystic, Byron's *Don Juan* (funny, tart and also a book full of glorious poetry), a biography of Byron and another of Coleridge. This is obviously my obsession, together with daubing paint on pieces of paper. Sometimes I have kept a diary, but consider this a mixed blessing. I will explain.

A diary is comparatively easy to write, providing you can remember. It also gives the impression that the author is perspicacious, looking on things with a minutely observant and loving eye. It gives the impression of newness, of brightness – almost, one might say, of journalism (but what else is a diary?). We all know what a day-old paper is good for: either for wrapping the chips or for use as bum fodder. The same is true of the diary. When I look back on old diaries, the only things of interest I find are the more general observations, mostly philosophising on the nature of things. The detailed actions of the day seem tedious and their effect is sepia, rather like a photograph from the last century. I think this comparison between photograph and diary is an apt one. In both cases we have a moment falsely picked from the growing plant of time. If one regards it as a separate item it loses meaning, looking like a meaningless cardboard cut-out. If one reads it, one is not filled with the sadness of *temps perdu* but rather with sorrow at the taste of the dust of wasted time. How lucky to be as Byron, using the observed particulars of his life and weaving them into poems and stories that forever change men's emotions. *Childe Harold*, for example, has all the intimacy of a diary yet embraces humanity. After a century a diary can become an interesting socio-historical document, but it does take a time.

This small detour about the nature of diaries is, I hope, not in vain. It leads me to the observation that, whenever publishers wish to commission singers to write about themselves, they are wily enough to ask for a book in diary form. By this subterfuge they realise that they will receive a book of journalism with an obvious structure. The publisher will therefore receive something piquant which definitely looks like a book and which will be long enough – a day's observations are, after all, as long and as tedious as one wishes to make them.

The Ring Diary

On 15 August I have been engaged to begin rehearsals to sing Loge in the new *Ring* at Covent Garden. At my advanced age of fifty-five I have good reason to believe that this could be my last new production. At this moment I have sung in three. The first was with Peter Stein and Solti in Paris at least twenty years ago. The second was with Götz Friederich and Colin Davis at Covent Garden about fifteen years back. The third with Nicholas Lehnhof and Sawallisch at the Bavarian State Opera in Munich about five years ago – a performance which was videotaped impressively by the Japanese. Now this new one is to be conducted by Bernard Haitink (a conservative eye) and to be produced by Richard Jones, a witty and intelligent iconoclast. This last is how he appears to be on virtually no acquaintance – in fact on an hour's chat and much hearsay. The designs and costumes are by Nigel Lowry, a painter and highly intelligent man and appeared to me to be sixties' brutal, that is to say ugly without a true commitment to ugliness, political without real understanding, facility masquerading in anger's clothes. This might all be unjust and plain wrong. It will at least be the most interesting area not only to a performer but also to a critic.

The history so far is that I met Richard Jones on 3 August. He came to my home and we began to explore each other's brittleness. I looked and made my decisions, came to my conclusions and he did similarly. We noticed how much space we needed and we began to try bits of influence. As a psychiatrist/analyst he listened a great deal, dropping the odd unpolished stone into the lake of my vast confidence and waiting to see if there were any ripples. I began a parade of easy-ego but affixed barbs that warned I was no man to be trifled with and, what is more, was as intelligent as he – maybe, however, in a different way.

This is the first opera I have come to with any fixed ideas, having recently had a good think – a rare occurrence. Recently, most productions of the *Ring*, the most archetypal of operas in thought, have insisted on politicising it – that is, humanising it, bringing the issues to the understanding/scope of the soap-opera audience. So all is about greed, power, selfish lust and romantic love. Obviously one of the ways of dramatising the changeless eternal values is to make them smaller in order that the scale might become acceptable. Another way is to trivialise them so that the inherent magic powers become fetishistic objects rather than those infinite jailers who beat us (or bless us) with their hands. By this method, the uncontrollable becomes controllable by contempt. Another way for the director is to distance himself intellectually from his subject matter. This attitude will get him and many of his audience a sense of superiority that will blunt the crude, inexorable, vicious godlessness of the score.

All directors will inevitably come upon the titanic anger and despair of Wagner. The success of their venture will stand or fall in their relationship with the almost Sophoclean nihilism of the composer. The music is a colossal daring of love, a world in which the inevitability that the personal ego must be exterminated beyond Hades and also drowns in the Styx on the way engenders a fury beyond most men. Wagner, with his Buddhist studies, knew the concept of eternal love, considered it important, knew the effect of its absence, which was destruction, but had no idea where to find it. (It could and can, of course, only be found with the extermination of the self, of that monster ego that was elevated to Pope, King and Saviour in Wagner.)

It is possible (or at least it should be) to produce a *Ring* which sees the music with eternal balances, especially with Greek mythological values. This is how I see it. I find that LOGE, god of fire (Greek), LOGOS, the forerunner of the Truth (late Greek), LOVE (St Paul) is the only character that might represent humanity. He is half-god, half-man, as are we all, though many would have to have their teeth pulled painfully to admit it. He is the demi-god, and as such sees both sides. The gods, on the other hand, are no more stupid than were Heracles, Artemis, Hera and so on – personalities obsessed with world issues, closed to all but themselves ranting on in predictable ways on predictable matters (rather like the gentlemen's club of today). LOGE in almost a Platonic way arrives in the second scene of *Rheingold* and announces that LOVE is the answer to eternity. So far, only one has rejected this truth and in so doing has enriched himself with wealth and power. LOGE warns and is ignored. Those interested in anything except the careless care of supernal LOVE will not only be finally destroyed (that is, die without knowing) but, even while living, will be visited by hopelessness, anger, jealousy and many more than the other deadly sins. Having ignored LOGE's warning, the cycle of the *Ring* follows its inexorable path. LOGE, who followed the progress with curiosity for a while, soon sees the truth of his knowledge made manifest. He resigns from the drama, to return finally. He then destroys a corrupted world with the refining fire of LOVE.

Such is my belief. Such is my hard-headed agenda as I approach ten weeks of this magnificent, miserable masterpiece. Richard Jones feels that the world before the beginning of *Rheingold* is the perfect – in this I read that the world before man, the pre-lapsarian world, was the ideal. As this cannot be the whole truth, I will put it aside. I like Richard. But when I saw him with his designer at Glyndebourne on 5 August I liked him a little less. I saw a confederacy of which I was not part.

My first gripe. My costume shows two faces. I said to Richard that this would be read by the audience as the old cliché of two-faced political, clever, untrustworthy LOGE. LOGE never speaks one untrue word. He is so clean, so patently honest in his attitude that those – the Gods – of far less clarity and more selfish deviousness can only see him in terms of lies – LOGE = LÜGE. We'll see where we get; it will be interesting.

15 August

A perplexing day. We plotted the first LOGE scene. Richard is a psychoanalytical director – that is, he listens a lot and says little. This, of course, pleases him as his thoughts are already formed. When I begin work (with no other characters in attendance), I tend to wait for the geographical placements. What I am really saying is that I don't perform, don't act, merely sketch in what I may do in future weeks. I find it interesting that the morning style (was it a style?) and the afternoon's are contrasted. I am not even performing. 'Why can't this be seen?' We have had two previous meetings. It seems that both were areas of 'getting to know' but not of listening. I meant what I said about the truth of LOGE. I am not sure Richard accepts that TRUTH is an area without argument or self. This, perhaps, doesn't matter yet. In slipping back to older performances, old habits, I showed an anger. This he seems to like. I do not. The cliché of the two-faced LOGE is still in the air. I will fight this unintelligent idea. At one point, Richard mentioned 'theatre of the absurd'. This to me is a concept as outdated as Beckett or Jarry. Both forgot or didn't have the wit to realise that, when absurdity is accepted, then truth will reign. Perhaps Richard knows this. He may be right. I hope this is sound, for, as I said before, there is no argument with R. Wagner – he meant his truth and will kill for it. Wotan's spear, an aluminium pole with a traffic sign bearing an arrow, is not only a cliché passé but also a symbol of fear. 'Which fear?' might be asked. The answer: 'That which we cannot control, that which is so important to us that it must be controlled in the safe area of absurdity.' I must mind my mind. It's his show, after all. We wait.

16 August

Was a far calmer day. I went to work on the Piccadilly Line, unlike yesterday. I ordered a book by Richard Holmes called *Footsteps*. I got to know Richard Jones a deal better. We share the view that Wagner is deeply nihilistic, a character who takes his calling and his whole ego and endless followers into endless perdition because he can't win. Win? Yes, win the quest for the source of eternal LOVE. RJ, with the control of the intellect, seems to be not willing to take the moral aspects of his view of Wagner into his staging of Wagner's philosophy. This I find odd. If you feel, nay, understand the cause of evil, why not confront it? Why not stand up? Why retreat into absurdity? This surely is the easy way out? Had a nice winner at York in the 2.05.

17 August

If you know or even suspect the consequences of life spent without love, which are inevitably evil, why fight it with a pop-gun? Today we will talk about my costume. It's Richard's show, naturally, and I'm in the place of the hired hand, naturally, but I will not fix this one up without a fight, or at least a compromise. Anyhow, there was no need to worry or 'project', as they say in caring circles. Today, we really began. After, for me, a rather boring run around mime's motives, Robin Leggate went home, the pianist, Alisdair Dawes, was dispensed with and Richard and I sat down to discuss the text but in reality to continue the debate about LOGE. Who is he? What is his function? What does he think? What kind of person would he be if he was not a demi-god, an archetype? The answer is, of course, a person exactly like me or, on the other hand, exactly like Richard Jones. (It does seem impossible to escape the self and those things that make it, those concepts, beliefs, desires, genes, impressions, histories. To be free, the self has to be torn from you, suck-pipetted to the Emperor Nothing. It can try to leave of its own volition, but this itself is a desire which prevents the desire. The needful loss of the self is a little like perfection. When worked for, it always rests just clear of the longest arm; when not, it will suddenly appear and kiss you. All I think we can do about selflessness and perfection is to keep our doors open to them when they decide to visit, and never raise the barbicans of false intellectual security.)

By the way – if you didn't notice – that was a major digression.

So I stumbled on in my mostly inarticulate way, talking of LOVE, TRUTH, and, as I gabbled, meeting an understanding but undoubtedly sceptical gaze, I said 'YUROZHDIVY.' This was exciting. The blue touch paper began to smoulder. The holy fool had struck a match. The match was a random recognition in the prickly brakes of our Semantic Wood. The message was instant. Yes, this is a good idea as long as it is not the fount of smugness, false holiness. No. It is the love of the effervescent now in all its aspects, with no planning, no reminiscence. What about a new costume? The old idea will not do. He doesn't care what he looks like, does he? NO. He only lives in the inescapable truth of the present in all its forms. YES. He is holy as every second is holy. YES. What about a dress? Why not? He is mad? YES, mad in his understanding, his knowledge. Does he have previous knowledge? No, he follows the Karma, sometimes with pain, sometimes with joy. Can you run with the ball? YES. Can you? YES.

Richard is a very nice man. I think perhaps he is also a good man. I will know later, but I definitely suspect it. Without doubt, he is a great thinker and a fine actor in a looney Aguecheek-idiotic-gulag way. With his angles at the joints, his Max Miller look, he not only informs me but makes me laugh almost to the dry cleaners. As you can see, spirits are high; hope it lasts. Stop wanting, you imbecile. Don't work at the *Ring* for five days.

PS: Richard suggested, playfully I think, that I considered the pause before '*umsonst*' (that is, the 'wait for it' mark, which implies I'm going to tell you something so mind-smacking that if you don't understand you will die) to be the most important sign in the *Ring* Cycle, and I agree. That the most important moment should be silence I also agree with, for what is truth but the inexpressible – the more talk the more nonsense. I think every concept grasped by the mind and spouted by the mouth is an obstacle in the quest to those who search. Prayer consists in the shedding of thought and consequently speech. I know LOGE goes on to enunciate a concept (LOVE), but he had little alternative being partially politically (control of the gods) in thrall to Wotan. Had he said nothing, the tetrology would not have occurred. The world might have remained in its paradisaical dimension. In the beginning was the word, said St John. LOGE, LOGOS the word announces it. Yet within the corruption of the word spoken, in it also nestles, in the same kernel, the meaning, the spiritual meaning of the word which might release the soul into a paradise 'here', and in 'here's' very instant.

23 August

Back to work. There were, however, some interesting things in between. A fine, refined, rather exquisite concert at the Proms was one. Vaughan Williams' *Serenade to Music* was performed with sixteen starry singers, of which I was one. That was Friday. Saturday took Hilly and me to Aldeburgh for a performance of *Das Lied von der Erde* – what a ball-crusher this piece is! By the end of the third song it feels as though they have been tied behind the ears. Sunday, I went on the train to see my mother in hospital at Barry, Glam. That was a bit of a ball-crusher too. (Many geriatric ladies asking for my autograph – they'd seen me on TV in the Friday concert.)

Anyway, back to work. Compromises are the stuff of opera/artistic life, especially when working with someone as fundamentally nice as Richard. The costume will not be a mess, but, much as the original design, the compromise is that the head behind the head has been lost – *Gott sei dank*.

Nobody really understands my philosophical religious view of this character. Why should I assume they should? They are locked in themselves, in their worlds as surely as I am in mine. I expect the world of LOVE to be available to all highly tuned minds. Sadly, it seems not to be. So be it. My life is fully in tune with the Eternal Spirit of that nameless IT which insists that I love indiscriminately and with no desire of possession. No one could possibly believe, but I am intensely serious. Well, we all have our crosses!

24 August

Returning, only briefly, to the *Serenade of Music* (last Friday's occupation), I read next day the thoughts of a critic. He mused over-colourfully on what the backstage intercourse must have been, how the dressing rooms were allocated, what necessary flattery must have been strewn in all directions. This, of course, is the desire of an opera queen. The gossip (oh my, what did they say, what did they wear, oh no, not that awful frock – wouldn't be seen dead in it!) is paramount.

This is hard work, and why not? As the characters in *Rheingold* have each their separate agendas (only a grouping around the concept of LOVE could mitigate against this, their perfectly loved solipsisms), so all the performers have theirs in various intensity or subtlety, depending on the intelligence of each. Maestro Haitink has his, I mine, Lynn Binstock (a nice American, a producer/dramaturg) hers, and so on. All that stops this from being an unholy free-for-all is the transparent fear, charm, weirdness, strength, weakness, intellect, ditsy logic, plausible brilliance of Richard. As a brilliant illustration of the idiocy of greed this absurdist comic view is winning and convincing, but as an illustration for Wagner's nineteenth-century mind it does not reach the starting blocks. However, if Wagner were here to see it, bearing with him the inanities of Nazism, political correctness, the heroic weak pins of the modern producer, all attached, he might well like it – as I do, really quite a lot at this moment. Let's wait. The YUROZHDIVY is still about, but only just.

25 August

Was one of those inexorably physical days, but it didn't start so. I slept really well and was finally rested. I then had a strange thought out of the dark. This made me consider the nature of conductors – Christ, conductors are a strange race. They are, to a man, obsessed with music. Secondly, and far less laudably, they are concerned with the others of their class. Thirdly, and most paranoically, they are dedicated to being 'friendly'. This means that they wish to be seen as 'ordinary folk', i.e. those who actually feel the dropping of the sun, the weeping of the moon. They are, of course, so distanced from the heroic world of 'ordinariness' that they cannot recognise it, let alone meet it or share it. Their vague passes of 'bonhomie' only serve to illustrate their painful amputations. Where life should show LOVE, they see Mozart quartets; where life, pain, the vaudeville of Tchaikovsky or Mahler; where life, LIFE, they retreat into the half-formed self. This is not an observation of Snoopy, nor Droopy, nor Happy, nor Grumpy, nor Wanky, nor Dumpy, nor Lanky, nor A.N. Other, but it fits them all like the perfect glove which palms the ego and simultaneously separates it forever from its source.

As the Spanish Inquisition niggled answers, so the six hours today niggled questions; shapes, however, of power are forming. The burying of Freia's doll with shoes, and all its echoes of the film of the Holocaust, is indeed a stupendous moment. Richard Jones is a good man. QED.

26 August

It does seem so hard for mankind to understand that that which can be expressed is as far from the source as is possible, the better the expression the further the distance from man – hence the Separation. The more perfect the object, the further to that security the quaking soul so craves and yet must lose in order to be free.

The problem with journals is that they are fixed. Day follows day with the inexorable steps of twenty-ton ants. Each day something must be written. My faulty but prehensile intelligence cannot deal with this state of affairs. I will throw off the shackles rather in the way I did with the SUN. One day – a radiant one – I said to the burning ball, 'No, you cannot command me, I will not sit in your beams. I will mole myself in protest.' I did that thing. I beat the thrall, and the sun still shone. This is what I will do with this *Ring* Diary. If there is nothing to say, then I will say it. That is much the case at the moment. Talk of heavy ants mirrors my mood. Blocking an opera is a dreary geographical thing. Feet morph into painful, toeless chunks, the mind watches the progress of time, wishing to be free to spend time with itself.

If only Wagner had written ironic music, how wonderful would this production be. It must be admitted that the feeble 'ping' at the climax of Donner's aria I can only see in such terms. The fact that romantic conductors have inflated this collapse of immense erection into the potent eternal phallus speaks more of them than Wagner. Is the *Ring* ironic? Most of Handel is, Handel was a German, Wag . . . shut it, you fool.

The box which is Valhalla collapses and is replaced by a star which begins to swing rather like a two-dimensional Foucault's pendulum. All the Gods chase it hither and thither. This is a metaphor of foolishness. It therefore works on its own terms. But what of the grand pavane that Wagner writes? Yes, it really could be ironic. I'm very much on board. I must play this character mad, hard and with no gestures. This is as far as I've got.

Two days off. God really does care. I've proved it.

I'm sorry to have to return to the subject of conductors. They (and the others) assume that music *is* the answer to life, the answer to God; and in having this shining, pulsing talisman they have to be wary of their power. The answer has been vouchsafed, they must therefore behave in a humble way. They should treat others as the Catholic Church treats some of its rather less than gifted flock. It is a kind of 'I know you don't but I'll care for you none the less.' What makes this attitude less than charming to me is the fact that they have not yet learned that music, however exalted, and art in general, is an irritating gumboil in Infinity's Nothing's mouth. Artists, scientists and little monkeys with paintbrushes, voices, pens, batons, brains, chisels act on a world, a part of a world so minute, so feeble, that the great rolling GAIA swats them as irritants on her fecund blind body.

29 August (Bank Holiday)

I understand that all the rest of the cast said they would not work today. JT and JH and BT and RJ did. Tomlinson is a good colleague and sings with fine black matt sound (not racially; how careful one has to be these days). Richard is desperate, cleverly so, to form a unity of style on this production. As the costumes cannot be disturbed in their soft brutalism, so all the characters must in some way be odd, eccentric. The fact that the bringer of truth should be seen in this way perplexes me not at all, for all bringers of truth have been weird men: men who saw angels in trees, and who brought the dead alive, and who were morality and love. Perhaps LOGE should be madly interested in the cracks in the stage, in the odd gold or silver sequin left on the floor – he would be if he loves and is interested in the bubbly now. So let it be. This started as an argument and has ceased to be. Richard's zany logic is tough.

I think I have found what I would call a weakness in Mr Jones. I think he needs security. He is a marvellous actor (at least with us) and I asked him concerning what he had done on the stage, how had he found it, etc. His response was to the point. When he'd done it and not liked it, he would have loved to put it right; that was the tenor of his answer. This implies that there is a right and, if this were the truth, then he would strive for it. This is so far from my lazy vision, 'perfection will, when *it* will' thesis, that I find myself lost. For God's sake, if we had two thousand years to perfect a note or a sentence it would be impossible. We are here, how imperfect can we be, and under whose hammer do we cower?

30 August

Was a confusing, if not perplexing, day. The theatre of the absurd demands, it seems, certain body attitudes. I can mimic Richard easily, if without his Godot physical attributes. I know it's no good questioning, arguing from a philosophical base. Richard has chosen this style. Beckett, I believe, was the most short-sighted man of his generation. What must be accepted as absurdity in his view (life), can only be redeemed in the loving of absurdity. If life therefore is absurd and is still wonderful and full of LOVE, then LIFE and LOVE are concepts in a world which is a miracle in all its opposed aspects. Therefore, absurdity is a station in a progress not of despair but towards LOVE. I can ape RJ's physical language. I can understand his desire for unity of design and attitude. What I still do not understand is his lack of feeling, his ordinariness about LOGE.

The place we work, the Royal Opera Rehearsal Room, is a quiet, good singing space that sometimes can be transformed into a musical Babel's tower. Electric guitars, didgeridoos, soul singers, rock singers, Chinese nose flutes, wail shouters, hair plaiters mix their worlds with the overblown but neat-exquisite Wagnerian conception. We must concentrate for hours on hours; any thought must be acted on and corrected immediately, obsessively. It's hard, but it will end. Sadly, very sadly will life also.

How long will my mother take? Weaker one day, stronger the next, eighty-five next birthday. Can't get to her; should. If should is achieved, then there's no more than an hour of everyday looks. Death – is it death? – is a slippery fish. It is in my pocket, it is in his dish. It's her, but when?

31 August

The attrition of the feet is Olympian. They do not bark, they don't have the strength. They whimper, then howl for release. The mind is not so vulnerable: it can decamp to a more interesting place, a vision of auction rooms, an old mother with chronic heinous infirmity, a fine pint oozing down a throat like the sweetest honey lost deep in the hive.

Richard does not understand LOGE and cannot yet. He does not quite have the lonely courage. LOGE can be no servant when he can leave at will. He can be no abject wit. He is an avenging god. The ring has been returned to the Rhinemaidens, yet he still purifies the world with his fire, still kills all, to begin again in the name of LOVE and the Earth (*Weib*). There are some parts that the theatre of the absurd cannot reach, namely and crucially that one step further than absurdity which needs faith, that concept called LOVE. Christ, Beckett has a lot to answer for. Life *is* absurd if you expect it to be anything which it is not.

Please, Monsieur Beckett, do not be downcast that you cannot have control. Rather see the godhead in what seems to you to be absurdity? Is there anything more futile than trying to explain your version of absurdity to Eternal absurd Ears? They cannot hear you. Don't fret, just throw your pen in the air for JOY and don't write again. Should this prove impossible, copy out Meister Eckhart and Lao-Tsu a hundred times for detention. As you do, please try to understand.

Yours

BOB

This letter will reach him somewhere between the Styx and Diss.

1 September

I have found an analogy which, I think, mirrors my situation. I have been asked to a happening. I have chosen – let's say only because of interest, forget the money – to come, to see what happens. (I am, as yet, alive and I'm interested in life's aspects.) I appear and discover that I am in an alien world. All the things that make me an eternal spiritual entity are absent in my colleagues. They all seem to be lost, wading through the molasses of selves or intellects or despairs. I am and stand apart, confident in my esoteric knowledge (which actually is the core of me). I keep spouting my vision of truth like a sperm whale on speed. Nobody can see, let alone understand. I therefore get bored and wish to leave. I must, because of my word, stay. What do I do? I watch with gimlet fascination every stupidity, i.e. that which is not of my temperament. I'm now detached, amused and interested. When the happening is finished I will move on. I will destroy the parts I hated with the fire of my disinterest. This is the view of the harbinger of LOVE. LOGE ergo BOB.

As these rehearsals progress I'm finding at the end of the day zany energy, the kind that in the old days made me jump, leap, want to do forward rolls. This must be happiness. I feel about twenty-four – I am as wicked and as undamaging as I ever thought I was. It's all a bit of a joy.

An incident today confirmed in me RJ's tact and sweet kindness. Peter (Donner) fell down and damaged I don't know what. Some producers might have said, 'Stupid fart, don't you know this is going to cut my rehearsal time?' Richard, although perhaps thinking a similar thought, was kindness, gentleness and tact itself. He organised, he looked, he waited, and when Peter had been helped into a taxi he continued. This is what I call sensitivity and care. I wish I could call myself courageous. I am a lion when I am called, when I am set upon, when I am asked heavy shuddering questions. But when I have to lift the dying, mop up blood, even pick up babies' turds in napkins, I wimp for the world and vomit, too, to confirm my quality.

3 September

This is in no way the half-point of this silly, lovely saga. I have, however, out of sheer wilfulness, decided to call it so. I look at next week's schedule and found my name not inked enough; where it would have been on the page there was a thing called *Walküre*, whatever that is. (Max knows, has heard it, even knows the story. He said it was like *EastEnders* when it got serious. I do not have his interest, and cannot be prodded into curiosity because the librarian Amgems is long since dead. Since that benighted time no one has cared for the books.)

But my intuition tells me that in a surrealistic and imaginative way I am a flickering part of a success (whatever that is). I am surrounded by fine smacking images. The spear of Wotan is a traffic signal which implies hopeless forward. The gold is shoes, endless-glitzy but ineffably sad shoes, which bear the memory of the feet that made home in them and which yet (before I drown under Holocaust imagery) nevertheless do hope for new feet to enliven them, aestheticise them. Freia is a doll, a kind of 'Mama, I'm going to piss myself' puppet who, at the moment of Freia's ransom, is covered by shoes. The cromlech so made is infinity-tragic.

Yet, in two-dimensional terms, this is a palpable success. Yet, in my infernally logical and mystical vision (not metaphysical – I'm not nearly scientific enough for that) I feel the need of another dimension. I am aware of being a participator in a cartoon (yet, to be honest, an adult cartoon). A sort of Fred Flintstone meets

Richard Wagner, or René Magritte goes down on Samuel Beckett. The star of folly or desire that the gods chase is a two-dimensional Foucault's pendulum, as I said before, a brilliant symbol.

You might ask – if you were stupid or bored enough – what the missing dimension is. I would say LOVE. When I say this I don't include the heavy, self-indulgent syrup that animates me, but would hope to include that useless part of life, that dearest part called ordinariness where a call of 'Do you want to use me again or can I put my stays back on?' releases time and its consequent tears. This is what is missing now. Perhaps this is Wagner's fault. I do not feel it is. If there is a fault, it's called fashion.

Richard is a good man, and I've realised that my new-found energy is a thing called mental stimulation.

5 September

. . . or I believe it is. I've not noticed the date on a paper; I do know, however, that my watch catches on my trouser pocket and changes the date in subtle digits.

The 5th or not, Monday was a creative day. I took Richard to lunch at Ajimura's, a Japanese restaurant where we, I hope obviously liking each other, ventured on character analysis. (We had previously banned Wagner from the conversation.) Can you imagine the composer's bones twitching in mad ossiego lust as, at various lunches and dinners, people discuss his thoughtless, bruised, veined, demi-intellectual views on life. A quarter-man in an eighth world is a big man indeed.

Richard decided that I was a dangerous but balanced man. He saw in me a seriously disruptive and destructive person balanced immediately by care and construction. He saw a deep nihilism balanced by light airiness. None of this I can deny. What I see in this gentle, intuitive, nature-metaphored man you read in these journals.

But bonus on bonus awaited in the afternoon with the coming of the Nibelungen. These creatures are usually ugly, twisted, vicious insects in brutal costumes. In walked now twenty or so young goddesses from a stage school between the ages of eighteen and twenty-one, who moved most supply in their rehearsal gear (ripped this, that and the other). They were the bloom of the saddest, beautiful, exquisite youth. All new, their skins shone like fresh peaches in a spring downpour. Their souls, too, seemed so new, so aware, that pain, if not already there, would soon colonise them with its wear and sense.

Such fragility touches me. My glasses had to be attended to on more than one occasion. During the cleaning I was bereft. I stupidly exaggerate, but such newness is moving. Life being inexorably strange, it seems that in the show they will wear paper bags over their heads. Well, what a tease!

6 September

The day, apart from the obvious rehearsal, was set aside for a lunch with John Tom who has been an acquaintance for years but whom I do not know. As we left the theatre, Ekke Vlaschiha, who is playing Alberich, said, or rather asked, if he might join us. So a possibly fascinating hour was taken in speaking German. Both of us make do quite well, indeed very well, but the subtleties escape us.

Ekke has frightened me shitless since Munich, I can't remember how many years ago. He is a mountain of a man exactly my age who is very German, and by that I mean he emphasises his points physically – not, certainly not, by argument. RJ told me the other day that he was a pussycat. If this is a pussy, save me from the sabre-toothed tiger.

He is, however, a very nice man and the best of Alberichs of my generation. He is all man, and I am at least 45 per cent feminine in my make-up. I'm sort of Dionysius whom women love because they feel at home with him. In Switzerland two lesbian directors eclipsed me 'Hon. Dyke'. I was pleased. Could it be that someone who likes all women (in theory), and who wishes to please them inordinately, but not to have them in the conventional sense could be called a dyke? Is Sapphic behaviour only confined to the absence of a natural phallus? I shall leave this here. The fact that there could be male sapphists does, in some way, tickle the fancy.

This buzzer having been put aside, I feel I must bring in some of today's work. I've decided to include two bits of criticism that arrive daily. They encompass Richard's ideas but they are interpreted by Lynn (very bright) Binstock and David (very bright) Edwards. Here is the first:

LOGE NOTES FOR SCENE 2

Bob – your anger and your stillness are very powerful, especially in a staging where everyone else is doing a lot of rushing about! Please keep working towards a lack of gesture and a quality of relaxation, so that the moments of action and anger stand out incredibly vividly.

NOW COLLECT YOUR GOODWILL TOGETHER! Richard feels your entrance is too weak and would like you to come out of the hole, with whatever box or hand grips, etc. you would like, and then head upstage with the definite intention of rushing to get somewhere.

Try to avoid 'Napoleonic' poses, i.e. holding your clothes, being too formal.

The best stuff with Wotan is him grabbing the air behind you, so talk with Richard about simplifying your circles, etc. and letting Wotan make all the efforts.

SPEAR MOMENTS – Richard said he'll settle now that Wotan grabs the end of the spear for the charge before '*Jetzt hör, Störrischer*', and that you should then squeak downstage of the spear to the other end, while Wotan chases you upstage of the spear, which means you need to set up the spear charge a bit further upstage so you can get by downstage.

NICHTS IS SO REICH – more passion

Was wohl dem Manne – really present it as a question

Des Rheines klare Kinder – less regret and more sense of how lovely they are, how much you like them.

Don't gesture before you steal your shoe, or we'll miss you doing it, having been caught up watching the prior gesture.

Take shoe from Fricka from behind her, cross BEHIND her to Wotan, but when you take the shoe back and LEAVE, THEN go between Fricka and Freia.

Ein Runenzauber – Richard has asked NO gestures on this; the idea is that you just give out information that is interesting to you in a sort of scientific way, but mostly of interest because of what it does to them, i.e. provokes their desire (actually, if you want it to go back to the Rhine – and how much you want that still seems unresolved to me! – you need to provoke Wotan's desire for it and alarm him about the danger of Alb having it, even though that is dangerous in terms of Wotan wanting to KEEP IT). (Eat this is approached by the wrong person.)

Could *durch Raub* be more ordinary, more thrown away – Richard's point about how little it takes to get big reactions out of these people.

Your stroll across the front – please take a good look at the giants and take the measure of their involvement before you turn away and go back to corner.

Make sure to take a good look at the greedy line-up!

Do you want to reconsider waking up Fricka?

Was sind nun Wotan – could this be less concerned, less significant? The sideways steps when the Gods come in work better without hand gestures, so that it reads clearly as distaste rather than fear.

Jetzt fand ich's – be more observational, don't use 'I am thinking' gestures (this is all so easy for Loge).

Doch ihr setztet – the anger is FANTASTIC. Feel free to use the space and move about on the ramp more.

Holding the apple – you can be more relaxed and not hold it so high.

The still chord before '*ohne die Apfel*' could be the cold hand of death grasping your heart!

(We will ask the aged gods to try turning downstage one by one, so be aware.)

It's wonderful that you are so passionate about Loge's value and superiority. Keep using that to structure your attitude towards the others and to produce the relaxation of confidence and LACK of NEEDINESS, LACK of GREED, and, of course, those fiery, burning moments of anger.

And now the second. In this you might notice a telling phrase: 'You could perhaps do something on this line: a sick or cynical gesture? . . . Talk to Richard . . .' David told me later that RJ's adjective was 'camp'. David, knowing how I would misinterpret such an adjective, decided to bowdlerise it. He knew how much laughter would have engulfed our small rehearsal isthmus had I reacted to the instruction. On the other hand, perhaps RJ needed a laugh.

BOB

Notes from scene 4 rehearsal 6 September

. . . *seinem Liebesgruss*: you could perhaps do something on this line: a sick or cynical gesture? Talk to Richard . . .

Please turn downstage to watch Fasolt when he sings '*Das Weib zu issen*' etc. so that you stay in the story.

Der Hirt ging auf: sing this beside Wotan, and then go upstage to the Tarnhelm.

After your '*halte du nur auf den Ring*' try making an exit stage left and come back on for '*Was gleicht, Wotan*'. You could then move across the front stage towards Wotan as you sing '*Viel erwarb dir . . .*' ending up next to the body '*das du vergabst*' and then go back stage left to lie down, perhaps in the trough rather than on the main stage (?)

Thanks

David Edwards

Somewhere, Bernhard Haitink must be included in this journal. I'm sure his time will come. He is the absent anchor both physically and Wagnerianly. When the real music comes (i.e. orchestra) it will alter all we have done. Everything must be heavier. The body/voice will be, and so the mind must follow. Sharp lightness goes ill when the composer won't allow it, and need specifies when it must.

7 September

No rehearsal today, but what passion in Barry, Glam. Mum to Hilly in Barry's Community Hospital (written on the train):

MUM

Frames to the right, crutches to the left,
Zimmered, rubber-clunked and squealed.
Groans, sighs, eyes drowned in memory,
Todspawn in milk pools streaked
To a care Neonate in my ageing soul.
'What a way to go, tee hee! HO, HO!'
(A joke as light as anthracite)
Whistled insensitive through creased old ears
As fearful as if pinned on baby girls

HILLY

But oh, my doe, should you so go –
See me crippled, friendless, legless
(From your perch gassing cheep to the cherubim)
Islanded in the toxiest gift sea,
Needy of death, terrified to will it be.

To Barry: what a town of boarded depression. I notice, too, that
new council buildings weave and grow like Russian vine. The citizens
anoraked, shell-suited, desperate, walk down those runnels called
streets.

   It was ever thus, or seemed to these cracked old orbs. Barry, what
a place to grow! What soil for the soul! Every tree winces from the
Western wind. Buildings crack with saline solution and ears shatter
from the shells of an accent engendered in extremity.

   From those days of manly swims in coffee November seas, those
gnashing tempest walks and those tracing paper ham sandwiches,
to the lust for the girl with the sausage dog on lead that neither
Montague nor Capulet could deny me, to these days of reasonable
reason, Barry remains my emotional sphincter (not arsehole, note
well – that would be too easy).

   I should never return, but I must. My mother stays, second by
second weakening, in a geriatric hospital. She hopes to go back
to her home (that council house in which five of us lived in armed
neutrality). She will, I'm sure. I'm also sure that it will not be
for long.

She should live with us: the species demands it. It is not possible. Hilly's mum lives, too, in a similar parlous world. To say that the two have not got on would be akin to saying that Ian Paisley goes down before the Pope – this is a pretty picture, I admit, but only likely within the madness of my fetid imagination.

My, oh my, age is not a pretty thing. Better to make rid of the self at the first harbinger, I say now. I'll not be so prompt at later times, I bet.

But there they sit, she sits, all alone, all hostile, or, if too ill to be, all fragile in spirit and bones. Writing with arthritic hands is not an urgency. Walking with osteoporosis of the hip is not possible. Seeing through blind eyes would be a miracle. Thinking with a brain never too agile would be obscene.

So I wait in Barry. I'm pinned on the cross of another's infinity/ deformity and will in a whisk so be. Is there an epiphany? There doesn't seem to be. I'll have to wait and see.

12 September

The first night is still a month away. This fact is as surreal as the production. The set lights brilliantly. Each character is super-defined in the harsh white and yellow lights. We had similar lighting in Geneva – it must be designer chic. With such light everything is hard, from silhouette to shadows. Blake, loving outlines would have been thrilled with this, as with the defined comic-cut characters whose searching inner desires are betrayed by their costumes and attitudes into prancing, whinnying ninnies. My tone implies criticism, but it is far from this. When I sit soft and quiet, not acting, not singing, not even thinking of these physical pursuits, and when I consider Wagner, I must admit that I consider the *Ring* to be a fair load of tosh – well cooked, it is true, but tosh nevertheless. Bernard has been reading up on Wagner's wishes and finds them regarding LOGE's character and singing remarkably in tune with my presentation.

It's fine to be back on the stage of four hundred or so shows. Shame on me. There's no health in memory.

14 September

I saw on the notice board something that angered me. Here is a letter I penned but had no intention of sending:

Dear Sir

Walking past the notice board, I noted that your letter explaining sexual harassment had been defaced with the word 'bollocks' and had also been ripped.

I would like to applaud the person/persons who made these protests. I feel I must remind you that the Royal Opera House is a theatre within whose juicy walls people live in a desire to express and represent the best of the human spirit.

This is not a workplace (no bank this) where love and all its endearments are sacrificed to a spurious equality and a desire for frigid efficiency. Please realise that care and kindness, the soul of human expression in the theatre, really exist.

Your letter is offensive to a proper human soul (the politically correct would not recognise one if they trod on it in their self-passage to misunderstandings).

You may call me follicularly disadvantaged, but I will stubbornly and with force defend my baldness. Yes, of course this letter issues from a position for which your direction was not intended, but yours is a dangerous road to schlepp.

There are some who have difficulty with their proclivities; artists tend not to. A theatre is thus enlivened by boys, girls, misses, Mrs, gifted sweeties, butches, queens, fags, hags, poofs, bores, normalities, all existing in an understanding, a bonhomie of fine liberated acceptance.

Please do not ruin it with the shackles and gules of your cyberborg world.

That neatly off my chest, I'll talk about the *Ring*. We had a *Sitzprobe* last night, i.e. a sing-through just with orchestra, no movement, no clothes (I do mean costumes). It was marvellous just to sing the music with all its written inferences, and such a relief not to have to oppose the score as we must do so much of the time. Bernard was v. good. He keeps it moving.

16 September

Today the fat hit the fan and the shit hit the fire. When I say today, yesterday was the appetiser. The seed of this passion? you will ask. I will answer: The Costumes.

You must remember that previously I have called them 'homely brutal'. I will not alter this ycleptness but will add that the emotional effect of such winsome crudity is an atmosphere so bleak, so hopeless that a seraph would dive from the throne. This is exactly what RJ wants. He sees nihilism in the *Ring* and, being the kind of visionary he is, he is right. (Read my piece on Wagner – written a year before this production.) Wagner is a monster to be pitied for his myopia, his sadism, his brutality and his complete inability to understand selfless LOVE. I précis in case you cannot remember.

BH, on the other hand, is a musician. Musicians have, with few exceptions, never been visited with the highest general intellectual disciplines (I now unreservedly acquit all real musicians, i.e. composers, from this charge). It also should be mentioned that their seeing power vis-à-vis plastic art is severely limited. BH is no exception. Sensitive, he is a fine man who feels music finely and within *its* intellectual parabola. So when BH is faced with RJ the concepts are so different, the solipsism so grotesque that only tears or what passed for them can result. Such I saw today. The catalyst (the costumes), primed to explode when the two were set together by the management, over-shot, over-splattered my expected fears.

The good news is that my costume has been scrapped. The new concept is that I should play LOGE like a shagged-out Philip Marlowe. A dectective working for the Rhinemaidens pleases me, even with dry ice in his pockets. I still and will not stop telling Richard that he cannot keep LOVE out of LOGE. He still nods, even at his lowest ebb. He deserves kindness, but I will win (this he knows), for LOVE cannot be denied.

LOGE is seeking the others' destruction because of their hubris. I'm going with this. Let me see if RJ notices. I'll say nothing.

27 September

Hil's birthday.

28 September

It has been odd, not rehearsing. It feels as if we've done it. We've not even begun. Yet these days of separation (days spent in other worlds, like entertaining friends at our place in Devon and chasing a mother – a very frail one, who has now cracked her pelvis – across forty square miles of Glamorgan from hospital to the same) can bring their salve. On returning to *Rheingold* last Saturday, the work we, I, had done felt like an old slipper – comfortable, well known and easy to wear. All fell into place and was neatly accomplished.

When I say all, I perhaps exaggerate, for Bernard still has serious problems with the costumes of the Rhinemaidens. Richard, commenting that he hadn't expected to have his views examined by such a thing as a committee, nevertheless consented to go to one. What the outcome will be I have no idea. But if I were Mr Jones I would sacrifice the easy grotesquery of the heavy latex for some of his brilliant images which will keep their place unnoticed in the hoo-ha of the *Mädchen*.

The mill in Devon is a benediction, a very present help in trouble. It bathes tattered nerves to newness. It occupies a world which seems so far from the fine idiocy of art as does a white duck from a warthog. This gentility is threatened by the widening of a road. An environment man, all long grey hair and science, a wizened stag, was surrounded by two pattering, neat-footed does. Their task was to quantify the natural fauna of our valley. They tested the river, they stunned the water with electric currents and found eels, lampreys and trout in a multitude. Then they sought bats and were guided by me to our attic. Here we have a batropolis. Here we hear the scrapes of dainty claws. Here we feel the air from wafts of unseen wings that prompt thoughts of ghosts. With the political climate of today, and foreseeing the future, I predict that the road will not be enlarged. I hope so.

Today finds me in Edinburgh. Yesterday found me, us (Hilly is with me) in Inverness, tomorrow Glasgow. I'm signing the testicle masher again (*Das Lied von der Erde*) and three times to boot. I always thought there was a distinct, heavy masochism in me. Now I know it's true.

I am reminded that, although being highly critical of my birthplace as a town, I did not criticise the Barrians. Once one has braved a certain latent suspicion they are uniformly kind and helpful – at least the few that I've met are. Its geography also gives it much charm. A gold, sandy beach is cut by a promontory, the other side of which is a pebble beach stretching the whole of a long bay. The easy, green, homely cliffs are filled with fossils – mostly gryphia or devil's toenails, as we know them. Valleys run inward from the sea. It would be too romantic to hope for the white cattle of Apollo to be calling their sanctity in the fields above, but to see the local comprehensive all coarse and brutal is as inappropriate.

But the world is all epiphany. Choose one, you miss another. The ability to see is of God.

One other thing. About five months ago I left the Garrick Club where I had been a member for close on sixteen years. It clearly caused some consternation, for various members rang me asking me to reconsider my decision. Why they should have done this I have no idea, for not only were my visits infrequent, but the input of my conversation at these selected times was negligible. Finally, Donald Sinden rang and enquired whether my leaving had been sparked by Kingsley Amis. I answered that in no way had it, but that my changing philosophy was making the membership of gentlemen's clubs less and less inviting. So that matter was finished. At its height, it was of less importance than an old mosquito in a half of lager. However, it didn't quite finish there.

About ten days ago I went to a drinks party at the National Art Collections Fund. There I met a Garrick acquaintance. He said that he had missed me, and I answered that that wasn't surprising as I was no longer a member. I rather foolishly mentioned that I thought the conversation there was less interesting than I desired.

Last Wednesday, a paragraph or two appeared in the gossip column of *The Times*. It mentioned my resignation, now particularly cold chips. It inferred that I found K. Amis and R. Day interminably boring. As I had mentioned neither man in my resignation, I felt just a trifle put out. I decided that such cold chips could never be warmed *al dente* and let the article be drowned in its waste-paper basket.

The Garrick was, nevertheless, full of those with much to say and stuffed ears, a perfect field for geriatric jousting. Most conversations were, in fact, auditions; most dialogues were aids to the pecking order; a chance to engage in mystic or metaphysical battle never once appeared in all my time. No, the truth was that it seemed a place of partially regulated egos which bounced off similar others with the sincerity and subtlety of dodgem cars. It was also a place where the deracinated public schoolboy happily regressed to Spunk House, Halcyon Manor, and loved every minute, the lonely wife at home forgotten but at least still a useful accoutrement in a man's, and what is a man's world.

30 September

As soon as anyone pronounces anything, the assertion is invariably wrong. Having lunch with Mark Wigglesworth in Edinburgh yesterday showed me that not all conductors only live within music. He has been involved in the infinitely tricky business of buying a house and having it altered. The builders went bust and he was left worrying. The concern prevented him looking at *Das Lied* for the concert at the Maltings which I mentioned some time last month. The performance was very good indeed, and led him to the thought that if you know your work you can retreat from it and let it play itself – a wisdom of insecurity if ever there was one. With this seed of knowledge he will become a great conductor. Having made that pronouncement, I hope that it will not be wrong.

I realise that I'm neatly mad. This gives me energy and belief. It allows me to see things that are not always visible to others. It's a lonely place, but it has a holiness.

After tonight's *Das Lied* it's back to the *Ring*.

2 October

Was a bit of a waste of time, which convinced me, none the less, that the four previous weeks had not been a waste of time.

3 and 4 October

This is what must have been called, in the early months of 1939, the 'phoney war'. I sit at peace in a halcyon, late summer in a mill that Apollo has only just left. I have forgotten, or at least I have been prevented from remembering, that in ten days the world will be watching me.

This anaesthetic of removal is remarkable, for not only has it taken the inexorable fright graph out of my equation, it has also taken the hypochondria from my soul. (As I say this, the mouth-roof, back-nose, itchy-seedings affirm their presence.) Well, so far, so good. But it's always the same, isn't it? One day alive, the next dead, one day a star, the next a forgotten fart.

I have decided in my slow way that I am a likely candidate for the world hubris award. I sport what some might call gifts. I can do various things a quarter well. I can write half well. I search for the spirit 190 per cent well – which is better than good – yet I am always within the spit, the gob of God's disapproval because of my ingratitude. I am always unhappy to be employed in something I consider less than easy. When it's easy I wish I was engaged in some other thing. This is hubris. Nemesis has not hit me yet. So being an aware man, and not wishing to try the patience of the great nothing too far, I bought me today, in Taunton, a silver skull. This, from now on, I will put before me on my piano, a memento vitae or mori to warn me of selfish excess or unawareness of gratitude. It's shocking to be so blessed and not be eternally grateful.

Today's news was of the Princess and not quite a major (could you call this a minor?). It was a story of sadness, idiocy, feebleness, touchingness, youth, hurt, care, but above all stupidity. Why do people believe that their hurts can be solved by any outside agent, whether it be a soul or a solvent? This is not possible. Whatever problem there is, is us, simply that. We carry it with us however and wherever we go. It can only leave us when we have learned it and accepted it as the old friend it is. It must not be indulged all the time, but it will constantly need to be. It can give us comfort, but only when held in good, kind equanimity. Sadly, it is only the proto-zimmered who can know this. God keep me from colds for the next month and a half.

Today I bought a book, *Secondary Worlds*, by Auden for a pound. I found it in a tray outside a shop. Wystan would be devastated if he knew. I will be fascinated. I hope, also, that the fascination will prevent too much self-obsession, too much dwelling on the possibility of failure.

I don't have a costume yet.

7 October

I have a costume and it smokes. My plea to Richard: 'Do not surround yourself again with chummy designers – sets, costumes, etc. Grow and feel the flesh of irony, taste the skin of that which you despise, don't make it easy for us to join in your contempt; make it hard, confuse us.' Of course, *Das Rheingold* could be called a satyr play, i.e. that in which the chorus returns to mock the gods. Mr Peter Conrad makes a fine academic point when he mentions this. What PC fails to recognise is that LOGE is not pleased to be 'no better than a demi-god' because he is an element; he is instead a true god because he is both man and God. Christ, I recall, used this relationship. As an element he is not immortal. As the concept of Love he is. Love was that pregnant silence before the bang.

What I say to RJ is 'Be your fine soul and don't try to shock them. I'm sure your natural goodness will be far more disturbing than anything you can show on the stage.'

This late, ungrateful revolt was nudged on me by a dream. In it I saw a Caspar David Friedrich spotted with the images of Miró. This is no sin on anyone's behalf, but it reveals to me an intellect of a Dada variety which I feel now as old as the '*Merde*' of Alfred Jarry. This is not the case in our production, but I feel it might subtly apply and feel I must remark on it.

(I realise that Wagner could never assume the mystic sensitivity of Friedrich and so I apologise to the painter – he'll know what I mean.)

A memo to me: Let me not forget that Love is FIRE and ICE.

RJ says that he should like to perform *Rheingold* as the last of the operas. I totally agree. That's what I call interesting.

This production is as a fascinating gruel, hungry filling for the thin intellect but scant use for the belly – and yet, and yet, the star is magical, the shoes unforgettable, the paper bags a spore of sadism and sweet sexuality. This production is ugly and real – rather like Damien Hirst's sheep. It is, however, also sentimental and madly saccharine, especially in the designs.

8 October

Showed a full rehearsal. It was also a dramatic rehearsal. Having played the whole piece – not an easy task – I heard through Ron Freeman that I should now wear a false moustache. As I am paranoid, and as I have watched LOGE become melded with the other idiots of this satyr farce i.e. director, designer, who think that I have not noticed or have become indeed a believer), I reacted 'ballistic'. I jumped, stormed, berated. Why? Because I find it hard to act if I don't believe. Q: Why make LOGE a smoking-coated gigolo? A: Because the design makes sense, it's unity. Because the characters must be alienated from the public. Q: Why do this? A: (a) the public are stupid generally and wish to be confirmed in their state; (b) the public must be awakened; (c) Wagner needs clarification (as indeed he does). *Rheingold*, in our time, can only be an ironic piece, an exercise. All this is acceptable, but why take humanity (LOGE) out, why have it all one colour? The answer must be that Richard sees no hope in this piece.

I must indeed have informed him that hope, LOVE, lies in the cracks of the pavements, in the pocks of the tangerine, in the ears of rabbits, in the pubic hair in the bath, in the forgettings of an older mother, in the serious angelicity of a dearest wife.

But LOGE remains stubbornly non-political. He remains outside, with his truth. LOVE is not denied.

So I said I would not play the harbinger of LOVE as a spiv. (He may well have been – who knows.) The man from on high – whose name I cannot now remember (I'm so furious) – doesn't please me. I'm quite sharp on auras, and for my soul I sense one here. Without my kind of care, how can innocent gold (RJ) find such solace in such dull metal I don't understand. Perhaps one is to die, the other to rise?

Opposites have always blended, but the get is often the lack of purity in the gold. As in a games match, the best will always find the level of the worst.

However (my pique almost put aside), this I predict will be the most divisive *Rheingold* and for my taste the most committed since Patrice Chereau fifteen years back. The images live in our show.

9 October

A day of rest. This Sunday, there is very little rest for me. I'm still in a turmoil, angry with myself for my piqued adolescent behaviour. I'm also so frustrated that I can come to no conclusion about this damned production. I am, as it were, surrounded by ripe fruit, but as I pick it and eat I'm rewarded with cardboard and worms. All is empty, but yet the shell glitters.

I kicked the good man yesterday when I should have strangled the other. Perhaps I need to behave in this way, need to produce devastating energy for myself. But it is selfish and destroys all in its way.

I keep returning to this subject of LOVE. There is none in this *Rheingold*, just a succession of brilliant emptiness.

This vacuum cannot exist. This, too, is what makes me sad.

Mother gets weaker and is now in a home near our old house. Hilly, the saint, is with her at this moment.

This vision is one of brilliant desiccation with no drop of blood or hope. This is not the world I understand, hence my unease. Tomorrow is the dress rehearsal, what am *I* to do about *my* look? They'll see. How am I to detach myself from the others and let in that small chink of humanity? It will be done – I must blend what I've done before with this and hope it will be seen to be good. No more thought now; the dress rehearsal is tomorrow. I'm angry and hopeful – a fair description, I would say, of this fine production (with the deletion of hopeful). This work has been a brilliant living nightmare of duplicity and truth. I am lost as I feel perhaps I ought indeed to be, because this is the intention in this scheme of things.

I am angry because I have given a mile of goodwill, have received sympathetic smiles and an inch of compromise. In short, I have lost. This reads as an hysterical tome – it is, but it's worse. Why? Defeat? Anger? Deep antagonism with the design suits me at the moment.

10 October

It's a mature prince of a day today. My doubt, my conflict is passing. I hope it lasts. Off to work.

The rehearsal was a triumph. When I use the noun 'triumph' it signifies a good achievement of work in progress. Everything fell into place. I sang like the demi-god I am supposed to be, with no obstructions between the voice and the audience. Concerning the costume, I suppose if winning was the object (which I hate to admit it was) that I have won (NO SMOKE). I have, at least, convinced some of LOGE'S CHARACTER. I'm certain that it would be good for Richard to find a different designer. Just for a change. I do feel that he uses the half-evil, half-brutal, half-colourful, unintelligent designs as a shield. As a dear friend, and I consider myself such, I advise him that now is the time to throw retention away. He is old enough, and the dummy of his chosen design is sucked dry. Richard is a man of deep humanity and love, a man of fine, yet different, intellect. Now is the time to cross uncertainties, to bridge, and see what lurks on the other side.

Bernard conducts the piece beautifully as he sees a piece of music. Richard directs cogently as he sees a piece of folly. Sadly, neither approaches the other, for one is all imagination but blind to the stage, and the other sees irony as a graspable entity. Irony, once owned, becomes cynicism. Irony is an open field; cynicism a political or philosophical or theatrical cross. The whole needs at least a scintilla of light or doubt. Neither of my two protagonists shows either; each is entrenched in belief and concept.

Tomorrow will be a *'succès de scandale'* in spite of both entrenchments; Wagner deserves no more. For half-philosopher, half-intelligent, half-craftsman, zero soul, he has come far. He is appreciated by those of similar qualities. Our angry-placid eternal-seeing Wolfgang loses no sleep. Wagner is no 'natural'.

12 October

In the Eagle Tavern in the Askew Road I met a man, an Irishman of seventy or so years. He told me he had come from a village outside Cork. When I asked him the name, he mumbled something in Erse. I soon found out that this village was situated four miles from the sea, four miles from the town, four miles from the church and four miles from the school. When I enquired the size of this village, he answered: 'Four houses.' This, I later learned, was four public houses – the village was inhabited by eighty souls. When I asked after the priest he said, 'He was a bastard, not a man at all. He would whip those speaking English in the schoolyard – even the teacher was afraid of him – and punish us for any lie whatever.'

He had never married. He was a handsome man with a fine, aquiline nose and grey eyes. I liked him, and was gifted with his experience.

There's a fish shop of some quality in the Askew Road. On the right-hand side of the cooking area they keep the crispy, unusable bits. I am Alberich in my greed for them. Unlike him, I have not yet gained them.

13 October

The first night. I've commanded Max Hughescoq (late departed, I do believe) my gofer, my eternal runner, to deal with this.

13 October 'no address but I do feel young'

I've been ordered by Maestro Lagrima, my creator, to quit my tiny mosaic deep in the empty fabric of the void. He summons me that I should write a critique of *Das Rheingold*. He recommends that I should write it as those gadflies do each day, namely quickly, facilely, skittering on the surface of the element as a whorish pebble skates the water. My master has warned me to ignore the gallimaufry of intrigues, bickerings, calumnies and joys with which he has arraigned me. I will be present tonight with ghostly ball-point quill in hand.

The evening was a mixed one, a success here, a failure there, a success there, a failure here. The singing was uniformly of the highest quality, the conducting excellent, warm, but perhaps a mite indulgent at times, the orchestra played well but with a softness that belies the piece and with various blips and bluffs in the brass section of which I expected more.

The production is argumentative and shockingly real in parts (I remember especially the torn flesh when the Siamese giants are forced apart), yet in others naive and crude. The story is clearly told. The music, however, tells a slightly different story. This dichotomy arises from two visions with two weights or irony. Less obvious irony from the stage and more from the pit would have made a considerable difference.

The images, at least some of them, will live on in the subconscious. The costumes are derivative and, I'm afraid, have the impact of an old and hairy blancmange. Lifting from great artists is always a bum idea, for not only has the artist inevitably been misunderstood but the pickpocket cannot invest the reinterpretation with any gesture of truth or plangent reality. Mr Jones is talented; with more serious designs this could have been a great show.

Max Hughescoq

Thank you, Max. Not a lot to show for two months' work, is it? So the *Ring* diary ends. We are promised a return in eighteen months. Let's wait and see. I'm sure it will look quite different when it arrives.

Nevertheless I've enjoyed it all immensely and, looking back over this diary, I'm amazed at the real passion it contains. Of such energy is life made. *Facio ergo sum.*

Composers Not to Be Trusted

As I earn my bacon and fried eggs from music I tend not to listen to it much, preferring the newer practices of literature and painting, both of which I practise for joy – except that I did sell two paintings. This confused me, not in so far that my direction was about to change or should be changed, but rather that one could get paid for having fun. I do of course have immense enjoyment from singing, but it stubbornly remains a difficult act, depending so much on the health of mind and body. So I listen to music infrequently – should I listen more it would be rather like a whore having sex for fun, and that would not do now, would it? However, music tends to have a way of impinging upon me, of surprising me at the most unsuspected moments, of demanding my complete attention when it so much as utters a whisper of a voice or a shard of a horn. I'm forced to listen, and adore what I hear. Now that perhaps is a bit broad. I do have very little sympathy for Italian music – with the exception of those composers who wrote before 1700 and Puccini whose glorious rot pleases me intensely (much as Richard Strauss does). Verdi, apart from the second half of *Don Carlos*, *Otello*, the *Requiem* and *Falstaff*, is a bit of a closed book, being far too political in his subject matter and not interesting enough in his harmony or orchestration. Those Donizetti and Bellini boys I can't stand. If you are a harmony man like me those endless, similar, tedious *bel canto* arias without a harmony in sight remind me of clotheslines with pretty clothes on them fluttering aimlessly in the power of the feckless wind. I know what fine singing technique is, but that too does not interest me with such music. Most music, however, gives me great pleasure. There are nevertheless four great composers who trouble me, who leave me uneasy, who force me to ask serious questions of them and of course myself.

I file them under the title 'brilliant but not to be trusted'. They are

Elgar, Mahler, Wagner and Britten. Each is a master composer, a genius, and each makes me feel queasy. Why I feel quite so strongly about them I will now try to analyse. I notice first, that with the exception of Wagner, the others were writing in the first half of the twentieth century. Wagner's influence was so great, however, that there can be no doubt that his shadow fell heavily on Elgar and Mahler. We know of Elgar's journey to Bayreuth and his impressions. *The Kingdom* and *The Apostles* were to be parts of an English oratorio 'Ring'.

The period in which they worked was one in which self-examination was to be treated with seriousness. Jung and Freud had begun to dig into the subconscious. Their patients found such innovative interest in them delicious and quite acceptable. From being in general rather ordinary, sometimes confused souls they were transformed into objects of scientific interest. As more of the underbelly was exposed, the more contented they became, the ego being massaged and burnished in the most pleasing way. As psychiatry made the individual larger, so the world became smaller. As the particular personal reality of pain became more acute, so the reality of the outside of the self became more generalised. The great Baroque issue which tried to make a synthesis of rationalism and belief, also the great Romantic issue of the lonely soul cast on the sea of fate, became replaced with the more particular questions of 'Who am I? What is the matter with *me*? What do *I* feel? How could they do that to *me*? Why does the "I" bring with it such pain?'

Of course the pre-eminent 'I' was always the centre of art, but at least in earlier times it had been coated with humility; most of the masterpieces of architecture of the fourteenth and fifteenth centuries are not signed but dedicated to the spirit of creation (or God, as I now waveringly call it) for fear of evoking some misunderstood and (misunderstanding) minority. There is to me something more pertinent in seeing the grand comedy of man (and I use the word 'comedy' in Dante's sense – that is, a story in the vernacular) and the individual's part played in it, in regarding the self as *the* centre around which the whole of life revolves.

However, in our times, and because of the advent (followed by the super-success) of psychiatry, art has moved into this new arena. The colosseum of the infinite is now occupied by *my* problem, the wheel of time runs not so smoothly as it should, the cause, *my* difficulty with *my* relationship, or in fact *my* difficulty with 'being'.

Here I have discovered my problem with most of the arts of my time (there are naturally exceptions). It would be less than interesting to plough through the plastic and literary arts, coding and quantifying those which transgress my personal rule (correct vision/philosophy). However, in these few sentences I have at least begun to see what my antipathetic feeling is to the four composers in question.

But before I begin, let me tell you a strange coincidence. I'm writing this in San Francisco, or rather I wrote it there on 26 May. Today, Saturday the 29th, I picked up the *Guardian* of the 27th and read an article entitled 'Pass Notes'. This is an extremely facile, silly 150 words or so which passes for criticism these days. No. 162 features John Taverner, the mystical composer *de nos jours*. Its level of criticism is of this exalted standard (I quote): 'Friends say ICON, critics say 'CON'. In this confetti are two remarks, both by T., which I recognised immediately were pertinent to the ideas that follow. The first: 'The best criticism I can imagine would be if you dug up a sixth-century man and asked him what he thought of my music.' The second: 'I dislike the way that *Angst* got into music through psychology at the turn of the century.' Thank you, Mr Taverner. This merely proves that JT and RT share a certain vision of the spiritual world. It also gives me a certain stiffening for the following. So, back to the four in question.

Let me start with Elgar. As a Roman Catholic, a true believer, he should have had no doubt with regard to the afterlife for his most precious self. What we hear in his music is quite different. Doubt is raised on doubt in a welter of indulgent indecision. I use the word 'indulgent', for that is what introspection must inevitably be called and it will fit my chosen four perfectly. Therefore please forgive its constant use. The tenor of Elgar's plea is: 'Please, oh my God, spare me from the fire of the pit.' His approach to God is the wheedling one of Newman. 'Lord, I am feeble. I'm a sinner, comfort me in my wickedness. Oh! that I might see you.' No, sorry – that's going too far. I know Giulini shows the same craven attitude to God in his interpretations of the *B Mass* and *Missa Solemnis* and Mozart *Requiem*. However, as many Roman Catholics do not show this whipped cur mentality

I must assume that it is part of Elgar's and Newman's particular psyches.

Francis Thompson, author of the poem *The Hound of Heaven*, shows, for my temperament, a far truer, more robust attitude. Here the ineffable, ubiquitous God is not to be desired. He stalks the poet, and when the poet will not listen he stalks him again until he has caught the soul. Here the presence of God is inevitable. We are for God, not He for us. Our very *knowledge* of the spirit is enough. We should demand no more. In our knowledge of love; we are in eternity. Elgar pleads for the resurrection of his puny self. How he would live in eternity he has no idea. Nevertheless he still desires. 'Rouse thee my fainting soul and play the man,' says Newman. He has no idea of arousal, play or being a man, preferring the masochistic whips of his self-created tormentor-redeemer. For his philosophical/religious feebleness, I cannot admire Elgar. It is fundamentally dishonest, reeking of the incense and unguents that disguise the stench of the decaying, imprisoned soul.

As with Elgar, so with Mahler: with both there is the absolute dread of the abyss of the imagined I. Yet like Elgar Mahler speaks, although from a personal viewpoint (as of course he must), to a generalised audience, an audience generally willing to mistake pathos for honesty. In such a perspective, a feeling of universality is experienced. In fact Mahler is shrieking at the post-Freudian fates from the most personal of positions. He waits, he whinges, he creeps – nothing of Job here, no sign of the inexorable love of the spirit through all circumstances. Instead, what can I do next to save my sweating, simpering skin? Can a Jew become a Catholic? Of course, one of our boys made it in the biggest way. Is a Jew or a Catholic more employable? Difficult one this. I've tried both kinds of Hebrewism – what about Buddhism? Yes, this seems good, gets rid of the implacable self. Or does it? In *Das Lied von der Erde* what do we make of the *Ewig? Ewig* – ever – with the shining stars of the celeste. 'Very little' is my answer. I see the twinkling lights of the Christmas tree, and hear the same feeble complaint of the loss of the personal 'I'.

So I find another philosophy that I cannot accept. There is a theory that, whether you agree philosophically or politically or not, art must be judged for what it is and not for what it implies. Eliot could not agree with this and neither can I. To be able to see or hear at all, I must share a belief. Having previously berated Derrida and Foucault for their assassination of the solipsism of the self, at least in terms of critical comments, I must here change my tack. In abolishing the self, they only do so in the canon of hierarchical statement. Solipsism – seeing life through my own eyes and feeling it through my own soul – is naturally the fundament of human, perhaps all, experience. All Derrida and Foucault say is that, if this is the truth, then who is interested in someone else's experience – however well educated, versed or intentioned? Ergo all criticism is void, therefore the text is all we have. Fine. So be it. This is my talk with my four chosen artistic difficulties.

I have mentioned Elgar and Mahler in the similar critical philosophical breath. I now turn to Britten, a composer born later than the others and one obviously more influenced by (for me) the pernicious Freud, and game for 'self-awareness'. (Jung I include no longer – his field that jungle of the archetype, his blood the spirit of existence.) To illustrate the difference before and after the psychological awareness of the self one need only quote Nathaniel Hawthorne's vision of how much, how close, how near the self of the composer or writer might be brought to the soul of the reader:

> That when he casts his leaves forth upon the wind, the author addresses not the many who will fling aside his volume or never take it up, but the few who will understand him better than many of his schoolmates or lifemates. Some authors indeed do far more than this and *indulge* themselves in such confidential depths of revelation as could fittingly be addressed only and exclusively to the *one* heart and mind of perfect sympathy; as if the printed book thrown at large on the wide world were certain to find out the divided segment of the writer's own nature and complete his circle of existence by bringing him into communion with it. It is scarcely decorous, however, to speak all, even when we speak impersonally. But, as thoughts are frozen and utterance benumbed unless the speaker stands in some true relation with his audience, it may be pardonable though not the closest friend is listening to our talk; and then, a native reserve being thawed by this genial consciousness, we may talk of the circumstances that lie around us, and *even of oneself*, but still keep the inmost ME behind its veil. To this

extent and within these limits as author, methinks, *may* be autobiographical without violating either the reader's rights or his own.

Rights, before Freud? Well, of course, but how changed they were afterwards, culminating in our own time in the cult of the victim. My argument with Britten is not of this treasured pain but of his lack of courage. I will, however, begin with his victimised self.

His choice of subject, almost his whole *oeuvre*, leads to the culmination of *Death in Venice* – the final public announcement of his sexuality. At the start of his career 'so-called innocence' is always represented. In *Let's Make an Opera* or at least in *The Little Sweep* a young lad is being mistreated physically. *The Rape of Lucretia's* 'boy' is the innocence projected on Lucretia and brutally taken from her in her ravishing. Even here, however Britten is ambiguous as to whether there was pleasure involved. Lucretia says to Tarquin in one of the worst of the plethora of awful lines: 'In the forest of my dreams you always were the tiger.' Collatinus remarks: 'If spirit's not given, there is no need of tears.' So we find in Britten an ambiguous fascination with the loss of innocence, the pleasure in its loss, and the pleasure in the taking. In *Peter Grimes* we are confronted by the so-called outsider, in today's parlance more properly called 'the victim' – a visionary with a fascination for boys, who can be both kind and cruel in rapid succession. 'Take the fancy buckles off your feet – Ah! don't take fright, boy.' The perfect irrational position of a sadist/masochist is thus inferred. Billy Budd is the story of the pre-*lapsarian* (well not quite pre-*lapsarian* – he does have a stammer) being destroyed by evil/Devil. Britten here is in the position of adjudicator/judge, his reaction to do nothing to save goodness rather to play it by the book – in other words to conform. 'I could have saved him. I knew it, even his shipmates knew it.' (Then why didn't he?) The answer is, I believe, lack of courage. This is an accusation which I will always raise before Britten's character and his lack of development – I talk now of emotional, not technical, development. *The Turn of the Screw* is more straightforward. Here it is the case of Miles and Quint, Flora and Jessel – little sense of the general cross-abuse hinted at in the novel. Britten, the victim of his schoolmaster, is carrying out his own fantasies. On and on it goes, with the pre-pubescent boys in everything, until he arrives at

Death in Venice. I will say no more on this now but talk elsewhere about deflating the preposterous membraned bladder called 'beauty' when in truth it should be called 'sex' or 'lust'.

Every subject that Britten undertakes confirms his vision of himself as victim, as an unfortunate knot on the lash of existence. He can never move on from this stance for, if he did so, his 'worth', his 'meaning' would be questioned. Without his homosexuality, what would he be? I see a composer with nothing to write about, an illustrator, a magnificent gift with eyes revolving in the search for inspiration. That he was the best illustrator of the best of texts was not enough for him. Today's culture of the victim as powerful icon also shows that to progress from victim/noticed to ordinary/ignored is the most fearful step to take, the false ego being obliterated. To do so, to find the true self in the destruction of the false self, needs courage. Britten didn't have this courage, and his toxic introspection leads me to my feelings of uneasiness.

As eager as he is to parade his secret, his loneliness, his lust, he will not face the abyss in the depth of his soul. He cannot cross the valley of the shadow of death. The man cannot love without discrimination, cannot visualise from an eternal dimension. As a result his music is brittle and shallow, haltingly obsessional and glamorous.

Wagner, on the other hand, has accepted the abyss, dared it, leaped into it and, finding what was there (the eclipse of the perceived I), has bloodily decided to stay. He bids us to follow him and to howl at eternal good. Wagner knows what Good is; he simply can't feel it. It is not in or of him. He states quite clearly at the beginning of the *Ring* – through Loge's tongue – that he who abandons 'love' is condemned to a dreadful fate. Loge warns, no one listens and the whole inevitable inexorable tale of idiocy, power and destruction begins. The spirit of God was known to Wagner, but never lodged within him. I feel that Wagner is motivated by a constant effort to become a saint, an effort that could never be realised because he knows the bite of the serpent, has recognised its meaning and lives close to its master. Being excluded from the Spirit, his temperament – not to be defeated – tries to annihilate death, the great exterminator. As Don Giovanni descends into the flames of hell with existential bravery, so Wagner refuses to admit his frailty, the weakness of the flesh against his pre-eminent will. But a Don Giovanni dies alone and with a certain dignity of belief.

Wagner requires us to go with him, to accompany him in his pain and his madness.

Marx had a similar problem. He too believed that God – because he could not feel it – should be excluded from the deep need of man. Thousands followed Marx, thousands Wagner, thousands Genghis Khan, thousands Hitler. Who were those thousands? Those who also felt a need which could not be satisfied within, those who needed someone to follow who seemed to have all the answers they required, those who, although sensing their natural loneliness, could not accept it. Even today in these anti-authoritarian times, in the fragmentation of authority, through the lack of threat (the Russian Empire) people still wish a leader, still love, still need the comfort of the group. Harmless but feeble, the Wagner societies still exist, following the leader in his didactic, glamorous but vapid quest to defeat the inevitable. They will find, as did Wagner, that death, especially in the face of arrogance, always has domination. The opposition of love is evil. Evil is what I hear in Wagner, and in such lies my doubt.

John Pritchard

One of the great performing characters of the opera, sadly now dead, was the conductor Sir John Pritchard. He was a large man in many respects. This I know sounds like a cliché but, as many clichés are, it happens to be true. He stood six feet two inches or so and he was heavy. I have no idea how heavy, but his legs eventually complained and developed some medical condition which made it difficult for him to walk. He was bald – a condition that troubled him so greatly, that he went to the lengths of having long strands of hair planted painfully into the follicles. This never convinced anyone. Neither did the most awful wig which he attempted unsuccessfully to keep in place in the heat and sweat of conducting. He was, most surprisingly to me, a devout Roman Catholic. (I presume I was surprised because such an outrageous character was, in my dimly boxed intelligence, supposed to be an apostate, a devil's disciple and hedonistic atheist.) He was outrageously camp. Very lazy, extremely musical. (It must be said that I was not always moved by the enervated nature of this thought.) He was, above all, funny beyond belief, generous to the greatest of faults, and kind. He also knew how to keep music in its proper place in balanced living. He was without desire and happily overjoyed with his lot. He was a man of the soundest philosophy. Apart from his hairpiece he was a man of subtle taste and discrimination, which makes the story of his death particularly amusing.

He died in San Francisco where he was music director and where he was to conduct *Idomeneo*. He completed some performances but passed on (on to where? I always ask myself) before the contract ended, with the consequence that the management was left with the substantial body which had to be flown back to England. I vainly tried to imagine what John's reaction would have been, when the official in charge of the move was asked concerning the inside of the casket. ('Would the non-living person prefer silk, velvet or polyester?') Polyester was chosen, as opera companies are always chronically short of money – but I surmise John would have plumped for the velvet.

I'm reminded of the sharpness of his wit in a story that comes from Glyndebourne. It is a fact that the humour of musicians is broad. They also love practical jokes, which they visit on those characters whom they particularly admire. There was a well-known arranger of popular music who had a sex change, moving in this case from male to female. The operation completed, the yellow, distaff hair in place, the make-up perfect, the voice high, she/he arrived for the first session after the operation to be greeted by a well-meaning note which said: 'Welcome back, Angela, how's about a fuck?' I state this case only to prove the general humour of some orchestral musicians.

Back to Glyndebourne. The opera is *Così Fan Tutte*. The opera is going well. JP is sweating but is also delighted. What he doesn't know is that a member of the band has vandalised a male porno magazine, tearing out a photo of a different sort of member in a highly aroused state. Ten pages further on, John will turn the page and be faced with this image. The time comes, and he continues to conduct without turning a hair. Curtain down, the orchestra can't wait to see what he thought. 'Well, Sir John,' said a brave band member. 'What did you think?'

With absolute aplomb John said, 'My dear, I recognised it.'

It is a curious fact that all stories – or anecdotes as some people prefer to call them – seem to spring from a similar source and are therefore related. This must explain the condition of one story begetting another, all engendered in the same archetypal mould of wary laughter and all concerned in the diminution of that wondrous leveller death. So saying, I am reminded of another wonderful Pritchard story. Loving, vulnerable men are the fount of good stories – the self-huggers and the cold invariably pass into stories less remembered, if at all. The stories of Bernstein are many, wonderful and outrageous.

The time had come for Pritchard's investiture, for he had been confirmed Knight of the Realm by the Queen. No more night starvation for him. John had the most marvellous house in the South of France, complete in every respect except one. This was not the fault of the house but rather of economic distribution or even perhaps sanitary awareness in the French republic. Anyway, the chance of obtaining the correct-quality bog paper in the South of France was minimal. So John had acted with great prescience and filled the boot of his Mercedes with rolls on rolls. When John was ennobled, the atrocities of the IRA were at their height and the police at the Palace were scrutinising everything, looking everywhere. Sir John waited in line. In due course the policeman lifted the bonnet, had a quick look underneath and then opened the boot. He returned to the passenger window and said beautifully to John, 'Nervous, sir?'

It was New Year's Eve in Brussels; a fancy dress party had been planned and was now in full swing. As a good Catholic Sir John had arrived in the attire of a cardinal. He had not even forgotten the biretta, and a grand ring winked on his right hand. It had been a fine evening, but as he had a concert the following day an earlyish night was called for so at about midnight a taxi was summoned. A ring at the bell announced its arrival. When John opened the door the driver fell immediately to his knees and kissed the cardinal's ring.

The final nonsense. The story is always attributed to Solti, but I feel it has such a timeless taste that it might be anybody's. In the pit at the Metropolitan in New York the conductor, having despaired of ever getting the Jews scene in *Salome* correct, is suddenly faced with the definitive article: all leads are in place, all is correct. So the conductor – let it be Solti – says with obvious great relief: 'The Jews, that voss wonderful, you can go.' At this moment half the orchestra gets up and leaves.

The New Glyndebourne

I thought it might be interesting to speak about the 'new' Glynde-bourne. Fate is the strangest thing (as if you didn't know). Why I should have been the right age, at the right time, to sing the right part in the right auditorium, on the right planet in the right galaxy etc. etc. is a miracle.

The new building, too, is a miracle. Visually, from the stage at least, it is a conundrum – almost a *trompe l'oeil*. It appears to be huge, vast, on the grand opera house scale. It rises almost sheer above the singer, like an unscalable rock face full of heads. It then banks and sweeps to the left and right, giving the impression of a warm and comforting glove. This is much of an illusion, for with the seeming largeness comes the uncanny ability to see all the faces – and even to recognise a few. The singer, therefore, plays to humanity on a recognisable scale, in an intimacy (not too close) whereby the audience may be conspirators in his plot. He can watch its reaction to his careful ploy.

'Has it worked?'

'Yes, it has.'

'Oh, bugger. Missed that one.'

This is a particular joy which is not experienced in the larger houses. In these, the artist is forced to select the person whom he knows is there and focus his darts to that person. Or he chooses to see the audience as a globulous mass, all political, all stupid, and wafts his message in that general direction. Or – and this is a far better alternative, especially to these short-sighted eyes – he sings only to his colleagues, and in doing so isolates that bloated queen millipede and makes the evening enjoyable.

The old Glyndebourne had none of this intimacy. Fixed to their £100 seats in the often smelly coffin, the audience was hard to see. Were there really people out there? No, that room was not pretty and not easy to work in. It might have been lovable to some (rather as an old wire-haired ratty terrier, with an underslung jaw, prominent lower dentures and halitosis to take the varnish off the Chippendale at twenty arthritic paces is to its owner).

And then, consider the sound. Just what could you expect from a long, plush, low-ceilinged hut? Some have remarked that it was like listening to a bee in a matchbox. This, I feel, is not quite accurate, as a bee in a matchbox, or any other box come to think of it, would make a huge – even deafening – noise if, for example, you were in the box with it. If you weren't, which is more likely, then you would either not hear it, or if you did you would simply wonder where the faint buzz came from. I suppose this is what the person meant.

No. The sound was not like that. It was more of opulence behind gauze, as if you had wandered into a fifteenth-century church in Italy to find it all covered with that green netting they use when they restore their buildings. They may catch a cathedral in it, but through it you see nothing, and the problem is you know there's something there. It's a bit like seeking God through the intellect. You fancy something is there, but you can never lay soul on it. That, in the most circuitous way, is what the old Glyndebourne sound reminded me.

The new is a qualified miracle (yes, I do know that miracles should never be questioned). It feels, especially when one is accompanied by piano, to be highly resonant. This, I believe, might be a snare or a delusion to new singers of short experience. With the orchestra, the acoustic changes dramatically. To say it dries is not the truth. The voice is still amply resonant, returning with some seduction. This again can tempt the unwary singer into taking it easy, not sweating enough. In my experience it seems that one must work equally hard in whatever acoustic one finds oneself, whether it be in a difficult house like Covent Garden, or easier houses like Munich and Glyndebourne. Here is a caveat for the future singer.

When I consider the enormous joy I get when I work at Glyndebourne, I'm much at a loss to explain it. Perhaps it is the gentle train journey through such good country. Perhaps it is the friendship of the chorus – those dear people not yet spoiled by the fingers of anger, of despair. Perhaps it is the bleating sheep, or the constantly curious cows, or even those enormous Chinese carp that slap the water of the ponds with their meaty tails and schluck at flies in the heat of the day. Perhaps it is the folding of the Downs which can call down fogs at the whim of a loose breeze. Perhaps it is the kindness, the true quality of those who work there. Perhaps it is the lack of annoyance, the lack of hubris, the great gratitude of the Christies. Perhaps it is all these things. But, as I think deeper, I do believe that the whole area is blessed with goodness, a good somehow engendered by those ancient Magi of flint and chalk who, at some time, blessed the earth and demanded that no rage, no anger should show itself. The landscape threatens exile for the selfish. This is high-falutin', I know, a candidate for Pseuds' Corner, but it is an explanation and I am sticking with it.

To return with a bump to ground, I must tell of a scene I saw a few weeks back. As I am not in the first part of *The Rake's Progress* (one of the four masterpieces of twentieth-century opera) I was mooning about the gardens, sniffing with hay fever and peeing in the wild irises, when I heard a commotion further on. I hurried, and was witness to a distraught lady of uncertain age rushing from the magnificent building holding her head and crying to an usher,

'Oh God, oh God, they have taken my Glyndebourne away!' She was last seen rushing to the pond – I hope not to be a feast for the flapping fish.

You know, temperament is all. Some need change. It gives them a sense of maturity, of progress, of the illusion that life is a linear path to wisdom. Others need to suck the tattered blanket of security. I need both and trust neither (and so does Max).

Why First Nights?

I do find it curious how audiences seem to invest so much in first nights. It is obviously most important to them to be seen at such occasions. It also enables them to chat away at dinner parties (providing, of course, that the papers carry the reviews). What they inevitably do not get is a good performance. It can happen, of course. But, generally premières are fraught events. The cast has been rehearsing for six to eight weeks, and is usually completely knackered. Six-hour days for committed acting and singing are not conducive to fresh voices and minds. Some of the cast will be performing the opera for the first time. They know it, of course, but it is not 'IN' every fibre of their bodies. I have sung 107 performances of Herod, but it was only when I got to fifty-ish that I began to feel I 'knew' the piece. There is physical vocal memory, and it cannot be forced.

I am reminded of the recent *Figaro* at Glyndebourne. There were to be fourteen evenings. The cast was almost perfect: a Susanna and Figaro at exactly the right ages and stages of their careers. Both were fresh but experienced enough to know what they were doing, yet not old enough to be relying on well-worked formulas. The Count was good, a bit handsome perhaps. I always believe that the Count should not be too attractive.

The Countess was the best I have ever heard. She was also funny (a budding Golden Girl) and so aware of the situation with the Count that no one could be misled into believing that the end of the opera would lead to happy-ever-afterness. The production was efficient, unassuming, clean, ordinary; the conducting romantic, indulgent, perspicacious, subtle – a conductor's performance.

We broadcast live to five nations on the first night. It was a good evening, but nothing like it would come later in the run. Just as a football team when first assembled has to look and consider and plan before it can function, we knew each other and knew where we all were, but we still had to look. At the fourteenth show we could pass reactions and thoughts without looking, knowing that the characters were there and feeling exactly how they would respond. It was marvellous – an ensemble, troupe performance trained to the last eyelash. To be with such a cast gave me a sense of unmitigated delight. I only mention this to illustrate that those punters who attended the last *Figaro* saw not only a totally different show from those on the first night, but also a performance 1000 per cent better.

Captain Vere

Having sung Captain Edward Fairfax Vere in Britten's *Billy Budd* fifteen years ago, when if not a callow youth at least a younger man, I was surprised at the extreme complexity of the character when I renewed his acquaintance in Geneva. It must be admitted from the outset that, in those earlier days, I was still in thrall to the Aldeburgh edict. This was that no sex should be seen, or, if suspected, should certainly not be mentioned. If the stage were suddenly flooded with naked boys, top-hatted and flippered and carrying riding whips, this would be regarded as the natural innocence, the irrepressible humour of pre-lapsarian putti boys. No, sex was out, and with it went an immensely important facet of Vere's character. I will not begin with this aspect, but simply ask, 'Who is Edward Fairfax Vere?'

Whereas before I had considered him a scion of his class, a controller, a wise man, now I was seeing him as a timid, perfunctory man, trying to come to terms with his role. What should he think? What could he do? As an unformed man, the answer was very little. With no weapons, how could he fire? With a class-shrunk soul, how could he be true to himself?

At the start of the opera (I am not now discussing the prologue) there is a feeling abroad that when Vere appears we will like him. We are aware that the crew love him. 'Starry Vere. God bless him,' they sing. As the structure of the opera stands at the moment (the two-Act version) Vere is shorn of his first highly significant aria in which he tells the men of their duties and what is expected of them. As we are short of this we must assume that the general feeling of benevolence for the Captain has progressed from his good, sensible, kind behaviour in his dealings with the men.

When we first see him we are aware that we are in the presence of a gentleman, a bibliophile, a headmaster figure of wisdom and patience. He shares a drink with the officers Redburn and Flint and laughs with them in their boyish denunciation of the French. 'Don't like the French – their hoppity, skippity ways.'

He naturally reacts with great suspicion when the possibility of mutiny is raised, but returns to his amiable thoughts on hearing the voices of the men singing below decks. He has obviously noticed Billy Budd about the ship, for when both officers say that he must be watched he says quickly and firmly, 'No danger there, gentlemen.' But also in his tone there is a tenderness that could be that of a father or even a lover. We are not sure, and neither is Vere. This ambivalence is the key to his character. He is one of those people who find it difficult to make choices, to decide on anything. When a decision has finally been made, it has usually been wrong. As the commander of a man of war, he is in the wrong job.

Perhaps he should have been an academic, or even taken the cloth. Somehow, some way, this defect in character, this weakness must be made clear. How does one play weakness? With difficulty, but always with courage. This is Vere's last sing before the interval.

The second Act begins with conflict and confusion. A battle is

imminent, also a dense mist is on the warship *Indomitable* – both are metaphors for Vere's inward condition. Does he feel a premonition that evil is about to cover the ship with its dark wings? Why is he so troubled by Billy Budd? No answers come or will come. His confusion is too deep to dig, too darkly prostrate for resurrection, too painful for countenance.

John Claggart is the master at arms. He is the law, or at least its short arm, on board. He is a pure manifestation of evil and as such is discomfited by the good, baby Budd. Claggart's hatred of Billy prompts him, with the help of a novice, to frame Budd. Budd will eventually be charged with fomenting mutiny. Evil confronts good. Where does Vere stand? With good of course, but he doubts his motive. He is not convinced that his attraction to Billy is only stimulated by good, but fears a more earthly power. Claggart is also attracted to Budd, for equally ambivalent reasons.

Auden says that 'The sea, in fact, is that state of barbaric vagueness and disorder out of which civilisation has emerged.' Vere is the spirit of civilisation and in no way could be called barbaric. He nevertheless remains in the state of vagueness and disorder. Perhaps in this condition he tacitly admits, in fact acknowledges, that this very quality has led him to seek his destiny on the enchafed flood. He is unformed, a proto-man almost made mock man by the accoutrements of learning. Courage is his problem. He has none. He should never have left harbour. He, however, knows that there is something to find, that really exists; he also knows that he has no idea where to look and suspects that, should he ever find it, his life would be ruined and he would be pulverised.

Vere dare not admit his darker self, and is thus impotent. He is unable to take any action because of this unresolved conflict.

Being a man of law (indeed, the letter of the law under which he hides), the Captain calls Budd to his cabin. It is in this scene that Vere's tenderness for Billy nearly escapes his control. His inadmissible passions begin to show. Billy believes that he is about to be promoted: 'I knew it,' he says. Vere, full of sentiment (not to say sentimentality), asks him, 'Would you like to be captain of the mizzen, Billy Budd?' Billy says, 'Yes.' Vere says, 'Why?' He is answered meltingly with: 'To be near you.'

Now the Captain has to tell Budd the news that he has been accused by John Claggart of inciting mutiny, and that the two will meet in a few moments. Claggart's accusation prompts a predictable reaction from Billy. He begins to stammer. Vere comfortingly lays his hand on Budd's shoulder, but to no effect. Budd strikes out at Claggart and kills him with a single blow.

Good has murdered evil. But murder cannot be excused. What does Vere do? He panics. 'God of mercy here, help me.' 'Beauty, handsomeness, goodness, coming to trial.' It is enlightening here to notice the same self-deception – beauty equals goodness – that plays its way through many of Britten's operas. The thought pattern is, I think, as follows: Because I am physically attracted and because this attraction must not be admitted, especially to me, I must call it something else, something which I can accept. Now what could that be? Why, a concept, of course. Something which is rational, of the intellect and therefore controllable.

This thought pattern comes to fruition in *Death in Venice*. Does beauty lead to wisdom? The answer: 'Yes, but through the senses.'

Vere decides to summon a drumhead court. This is quite the wrong decision, for although the enemy is near it is not that near. There is no need to rush judgement. A better action might have been to place Budd in irons below and wait until the *Indomitable* anchored in home waters before the full trial. But, like an old lady in a storm, Vere does not know which way to turn. He is the only witness – at least, if he takes God out of the equation. The officers say that they have no choice. Budd must be executed. But before they make the final decision, they make an ultimate plea to Vere. 'Sir, help us. Grant us your guidance,' they ask. Vere's reaction again is typical. 'No, do not ask me, I cannot,' he replies. Just as the lamb before the shearer, Vere is the one who openeth not his mouth.

In the epilogue, Vere, now a defeated and broken man, admits, 'I could have saved him, he knew it, even his shipmates knew it.' Then why did he not? As previously mentioned, he uses the law to excuse himself. We know that he is incapable of decisions. But could it not be that, if Budd had lived, Vere would have been brought face to face again and again with that emotion that he could not admit to himself?

Vere then retreats into the religious world, into spiritual cliché, for his salve. With an obvious intellectual connection the Captain sees

Budd as Christ. Billy has saved Vere by his hanging, his sacrifice. As Christ dies for man, Billy has died for Vere, and in so doing has given this racked soul a modicum of peace. 'The love that passes understanding has come to me.' Is Vere whistling, 'Eternal Father, strong to save' into the teeth of a tempest? I tend to believe that he is.

The vacillating Vere is a joy to sing. It is neither too high nor too low and the words are set with a fastidiousness that make them a pleasure to make sense of. The part is also fascinating to play. The individual scenes are the perfect length for the maximum impact. The character, I feel, must be acted tightly and rigorously controlled, so fiercely that nothing – or at least only a wisp – of his inner conflict is apparent. The surface must be calm. Through this glaze the fierce, bloody inner wars should be glimpsed as painful, shadowy dreams.

There has been much discussion concerning the meaning of the thirty-four bare chords which Britten uses as the interlude in which Vere conveys his dreadful message to Budd. The chords are cunningly divided between the various sections of the orchestra: tutti, woodwinds, brass, strings, horns alone. The speculation has centred on Christ's age at his death, alas only thirty-three. This thought was the outcome of a sharp musical historian making a direct comparison between the Britten and the ten bare chords and single notes that Berlioz uses to show the years in which Christ grew to wisdom. Another speculation was that perhaps Peter Pears had been thirty-four when he sang it first. This also is not true. The answer, I believe, is this: in 1947 Britten became acquainted with Herman Melville's novella *Billy Budd* and decided it would make an opera. Britten was born in 1913, and thirteen from forty-seven is thirty-four. Britten was thirty-four. His age at the time of the conception of the opera is therefore entered into the score, and is a delicious conceit.

Academe

Max (it's quite interesting how this name pops up in female erotica, but very rarely do you meet a daytime Max. What is it about Max? I suppose the name assumes girth and, for those books which are meant to be read with one hand, this is a must.) Anyway, Max, as you must now know, is, I think, my archetypal singer who has bestridden all ages like a bronze colossus, suffering pain, hardship, toil and the occasional felicity which has eased his passage.

Some high academics in various lands have noticed that Max is not as young as he was (he has been 'at it' for eternity, so that's not too surprising). Also that, by now, he has certain qualifications – name and the odd honorary degree – which seem to make him ideal to be the principal of high institutions.

In those days the political imperative was one of market forces, that quaint idea where worth was defined by productivity and excellence, by popularity and cupidity. How much could Stravinsky's *Symphony of Psalms* be worth? How many records sold? Really, not 20 million? Can't be much good, then? So Max was asked to ease himself into two fine institutions in this Alice in Wonderland age. (Except, of course, I do a disservice to Alice as her journeys are intellectually secure, even if reversed.)

'Come on, Max, help us out, you're the very man. You'll love it.'

Max, a little flattered that a new world appears to be opening to him, and also concerned about the future (imbecile), accepts.

What did he wear that day? What does the eternal singer wear? Never a suit, that's sure. Too constricting for the body and psyche. Never a tie? Well, sometimes, but only the example that shows slight artistic vision, a modicum of eccentricity.

What was his attitude? That of a golden visitor from another planet; someone sure of his reputation, easy charm, grace in his

skin, pleasurably smug. We are discussing these sartorial aspects of
Max to show that he was pleased not only with himself, but with his
past, his life, his prospects.

With firm, confident tread he entered the old, slightly forbidding
conservatoire. Perhaps the word 'forbidding' ought to be explained.
No. 'Disapproving' is, perhaps, a better description; 'penal' would
be going too far. Yet the building, with all its elegance, was covered
with a dark hue of subdued dissatisfactions. It welcomed Max with
disdain and anger. It has seen better days. The paintwork will soon
need attention, the varnish of the banisters chipped by many rings. A
haughty old female toff with her hat not quite straight and smudged
lipstick would have felt comfortable. Max, who wasn't wearing a hat
and whose make-up was perfect, didn't.

The people Max met were a strange lot. The professors, for this
is what they called themselves, and the big bosses were besuited
and betied. The colours of these garments ran through that gaudy
section of the spectrum, the light dark grey, via the dark grey to
dark blue. There were no patterns to be seen, apart from a daring
stripe on a tie. White shirts were *de rigueur*. Max could have been
entering a bank, or an accountants' seminar, or even a convention
of headmasters; but a music conservatory? *Please.*

The students Max found to be as they had always been: messy,
pretty, spotty, vulnerable, gentle, hurtable, obsessed with sex and
the everlasting self, and talented, fresh-voiced, cliché-ridden – just
as they had been in the sixteenth century; except now, perhaps, they
were a little more protected from those hard elements penury and
disappointment (at least, while still immured within those noble,
red-brick walls).

Max, a sensitive guy with high-tuned antennae, is sitting drinking
a cup of coffee (which always gives him an instant headache –
why does he do it?). His nerve endings twitch, he is receiving.
As the message becomes clearer he is aware of an atmosphere,
an uncomfortable one. The building has no peace. The people
within are not happy, are not relaxed, are troubled. There are
whispers in the air, conflicting whispers. There is schizophrenia
abroad. 'What are we supposed to be?' comes the message. 'What
is our function?' 'Are we an academic, intellectual institution, which
should have an old university's prowess, or are we a performing
academy where we will teach excellence in performance, where

we will find future stars with indestructible technique and searing communicative power?'

Max wonders why this Janus attitude should prevail, why this institution cannot be the trainer only of future performers. Why not just give up the academic side? After all, most musicians are no good at it and it helps them so very little as performers.

An answer came to him. He looked to the top positions and found them to be occupied by university-trained, joyous disciplinarians who had emerged from their various alma maters with good first-class degrees or upper seconds. While at university they had been college musicians, playing the chapel organ, conducting amateur student choirs, conducting (badly) various pickup chamber bands, but never, ever so remotely, professional musicians. In these people there was a carefulness, a cake-and-eat-it attitude which prevented them giving themselves to the performers' life with its uncertainties, worries and blinkered commitment.

The academic colleges and conservatoires had emerged from the university system and had no idea of the way to change to become their destiny. They were like amphibians – at home in both environments. Yet, unlike the animals, they were conscious of a better life awaiting on either side of the divide. He found them a halfway house, all unity on the surface but confused in the soul.

Max also found the teachers to be a strange lot with two or three notable exceptions, especially among the singing staff. They were 'failed' performers. By that, Max meant they had been singers on a provincial level but had never progressed to the tough, foreign fields of world competition. Consequently, this experience could be compared to that of a small-town councillor lost in the deep labyrinth of Euro or international politics. To this parishioner aspect was added the fact that most of these careers had been brought to an abrupt end more than thirty years before, and since that time they had willingly become prisoners of the institution and so also of all the vicious political in-fighting.

Max, being a sensitive chap (as mentioned before), noticed that teachers, on the whole, were a rather possessive group. Rather aping the Svengali/Trilby relationship, each close to his favoured student as a possession, and each to his teaching technique as holy writ. A public institution was used as a private consultation.

He noticed, too, that they were still promoting singing attitudes which were fifty years behind the times. Their pupils arrived at auditions (as potential artists) looking like the siblings of tailors' dummies: white-shirted, tie tightly fixed, tight suit, tightly buttoned on the middle of the three. (He remembered once discussing the potential of a new singer with a respected caryatid of the musical firmament. 'What do you think of him?' said Max. The answer zinged back through tight lips: 'He's the sort who sings with his jacket undone.' Such an attitude really describes the prevailing climate of behaviour, dress and singing nous. A fly in amber could not illustrate the situation more exactly.)

What they taught was also like a wan ghost of the past – powerful if one wished to believe, non-existent if one didn't. Between the 1860s and 1950s, the way that most professional singers sweated for their crust was through the music societies of the land, those artistic neons of the manufacturing society, whereby 'owner of t'mill' made pecuniary peace with his philistinism. Not before being accused of being anti-Victorian, Max must hasten to add that this tendency is alive and super-well and, thankfully, shovelling coal into the boilers of today's artistic engine. A near but tiny neighbour of the immense choral concert was the perfectly formed recital. In this most exquisite of atmospheres, the leading singers of the time would utter as priests. Eyes closed (no doubt with the words printed on the insides of the eyelids), they would intone the latest French confection or Gothic *Lied*, or even perhaps an easy bouquet from Italy.

Current teaching was imprisoned in this past. It was a concoction of sentimentality, insensitivity and arrogance. Such Max noticed. As a man for all time, he also knew today's world. Could it be farther from prevailing norms? He thought not.

'What did they teach?' Max asked himself, inquisitively. Naturally enough, the students were taught to prepare themselves for a future so misread that it was already half a century behind. They were taught those techniques, ideas and attitudes that would have helped them to satisfying careers on the oratorio platform or the perfumed islands of recitals. The teachers were now so distanced from the real world of modern performance that they had no idea that most of the choral societies had collapsed and that only three singers in the world could fill a hall for a recital – that now opera was the buzz activity, the bread and butter of the business. Still training their credulous pupils to believe that they had to specialise, to be concert singers, lieder singers and perhaps opera singers, they had totally misunderstood a world which demanded that singing was simply singing and that, if you were a complete and competent singer, you would be expected to do it all.

Max found this antediluvian attitude somewhat amusing, but also sad.

Mr Hughescoq (ABC, Hons PQR, AZPS, XDS (failed)), then began to look at the students' curricula. How did they fill the hours? He was amazed, for the most surprising thing was that very little time was devoted to the study of vocal technique or learning to sing. Wherever he looked there were small power bases.

He noticed that the principal study, in this case singing, was allocated a scroogy ninety minutes. He was aware too, that a thing called 'coaching' occupied thirty minutes of a pregnant week. He was prompted to consider why both a teacher of voice and a coach were needed. This desensification implied that either the teacher knew nothing of music (i.e. couldn't play the piano) or had scant ideas of drama or dramatising; was, in fact, thick to the obvious needs of performance. Could this be a penumbral memory of those days when singers depended on this kind of help? Max thought it could.

He looked further and found a subject called 'Movement'. It was destined to occupy ninety minutes (the same amount of time as vocal technique, you've noticed). In those far-off now halcyon days he had spent at the court of Urbino, 'movement' implied the neat departure effected after the wily shagging of an aristocrat's wife, or the sharp exit taken when the comptroller of moneys had sent him double. What was this 'movement' of today? It was, he quickly learned, no more than a 'Feel good together, luvvies', kind of 'Nipponese togetherment' where the stressed soul could become unloosed and breathe, where self could be subsumed into an early Third Reich cult of the body which now might be seen as political social consciousness. These classes, he found, were ill attended, the natural temperament of the singer being individual and ego-obsessed.

He saw that sixty minutes a week was devoted to French, sixty minutes to Italian. This, he knew, was not the learning of the languages in any grammatical way, rather the learning of the pronunciation of them. He admitted it was essential, yet he could not understand why this job was not undertaken by the singing professors. It was a difficult task, he had to concede, but surely not impossible at this comparatively early educational stage? Where was the German tuition? Was the language too easy, or were the prospectus makers still aware of the wars with the Bosch?

Then there were sixty minutes allocated to drama. He presumed that drama's function was to open innocent eyes to the human tensions present in all music, to convince the students that, if transferred to the music in hand, their worries, excitements, love affairs and hatreds would prove invaluable. But drama alone! Max knew that there would be no need for such a class, if even the simplest of Schubert songs was taught as if it were an opera scene, with every ounce of dramatic colour spotted and lit.

Ninety minutes was given to that sentimental, caramel collection called French song. Ninety minutes learning to breathe low-octane boudoir bourgeois air, perhaps never to sing in public, but surely highly pleasing to sing at home and to admire the exquisite, but small, tone of one's voice.

Ninety minutes was given over to lieder – surely not long enough when one considers the enormous literature of supreme importance. While considering French song, Max was irresistibly reminded of the critics. Why was it, he thought, that they always commented, most unfavourably, on French pronunciation? Were they all fluent in the language? Or was it all conceit and fancy – a sort of souvenir of A-level French which they did awfully well with. They never commented on German – strange, that!

Max knew that the system was wrong. The actual activity of learning to sing had been hi-jacked by small, self-interested groups and made to show obeisance to fashionably correct theory. He tried to make suggestions. He even succeeded in reducing the ludicrous time spent on movement. But to change the whole proved too much. The lumbering tanker could only turn by three degrees every twenty-five years.

What was Max's ideal? First, he would carefully vet the intake. There would be no room for the half-talented. Even if fewer students meant fewer professors, so it would be. Second, he would carefully vet the said teachers. Most were simply not good enough, being out of touch, insensitive, possessive and dead to the dramatic implications of their so-called art. He would go to the Secretary of State and suggest that a new honour be created for the profession. If accepted, the recipient would have to teach part of the year in an institution. So the academies and colleges would be visited by living, doing, real artists and would be brought kicking into the twenty-first century.

These fine teachers would teach all from their gold experience. They would insist on the operative quality of all music; even in a string quartet, dramatic incident would be found. They would produce a Brahms song using props, furniture, people to create the drama. They would show how real movement is inexplicably bound to internal incident, to sensitivity and awareness of mood. They would *only* concentrate on technique and meaning. Such a world, Max knew, was an ideal which could never be achieved in such enormously self-satisfied places, could never breathe in the world where the second-rate was king. Tedious tradition and self-righteous certainty are found at the roots of our very tree; while these remain, the plant will not grow. For as long as the intellect and excellence remain cocooned in posture, our football, rugby, cricket, art, films and scholarship will rest comfortable within the parameters that we have skilfully constructed to protect us from change and the sheer devil of love and experiment.

Why the Vernacular?

Some years ago I walked into an opera house in Copenhagen. Max was there, too, I seem to remember. The opera being performed that evening was called *Figaro's Brillup*! On considering the performance later I found it perfectly adequate: the music was played well from stage and pit; the designs were adequate. I was, however, baffled. The composer, Mozart, could be distinguished – but only just – through the bloops, gurgles and musical plumbing of the language. It was as if I was listening to his music on a far-off planet. I could visualise the composer in a spacesuit sitting at his console, writing with the aid of floppy discs in their ultimate form. It was Mozart, and yet it wasn't Mozart. What, then, was it? It was Danish. The vernacular had transformed one art form into another. I thought this a tragedy, as did Max.

A few years later in Hamburg, I willingly paid to listen to an opera by Verdi called *Der Troubadour*. This was to be a German version of *Il Trovatore*. The German language is poetic, sometimes beautiful and wonderful to sing. It is best when concerned with those very German values of psyche, mythology and mysticism. It suits the discussion of these concepts like a glove. It commands, it demands, it can be romantic and winning and purposefully soft. It is, however, not fluid and refuses, stubbornly, to adapt itself to an Italian *bel-canto* line. Der Troubadour as I heard it reminded me most unhealthily of Bellini's *Madonna of the Meadows* with a Lukas Cranach virgin grasping centre stage.

Then again, when Max was singing the *St Matthew Passion* in an English translation, specifically, one might almost say obsessively, tailored to accommodate *all* of Bach's notes, he confided to me that his impression was not of Bach at all, but rather of Elgar.

I think it is reasonable to pose two questions concerning the language that opera uses. The first: Why is it thought necessary to use the vernacular at all? The second: Why does such usage completely change the soul of the piece? (There is a third question which concerns the labour of those singers who learn, let's say, *Die Zauberflöte* in English, and then have to relearn it in German so that it might be more useful to them.)

One of the most obvious reasons for translating libretti into the language of the people is that by so doing they may better understand the drama. This attitude was prevalent in those liberal days of the sixties and early seventies, when the political correctness of the time presumed not only that 'Great Art' was for everyone, but also that Mr Everyone should be helped on the way up Parnassus. That everyone was not consulted on whether such an ascent might please him never occurred to the artistic social engineers. They went further and decided that if opera was sung in English the elitism of the form would be countered, and concluded that vulnerable Johannes Publikum would no longer feel the sharp draught of social and artistic deracination.

This old *canard* concerning the elitism of opera has always been helped into the air with more hope than intellect. The truth, as it seems to me, is that all 'great art' requires from those who practise or love it is a special gift – or perhaps, not wishing to go so far, at least an aptitude. To assume that art should be understandable to all is similar to the assumption that I might have challenged for the Olympic title at one hundred metres, or that Max might have kept goal in the World Cup. (This is being unfair to Max for, indeed, he was a goalie, his most insistent memory being that match in 1500 in the stadium in Verona when Michelangelo, the right winger, broke his nose against Max's left stanchion. Leonardo, who was at the end of his footballing prowess and playing for Roma, was seen by Max to trip Michelangelo, snigger as he broke his nose, and mutter, 'That'll queer your pitch with the boys!' But I think I digress.)

No. We are all unique and devastatingly so. Social engineers will always hope, indeed believe, that this is in fact not the case. For in such assumptions their job is made easier and their grail more simply garnered. The natural anarchy of the individual constantly scuppers such utopian plans.

On a more practical level it was never even remotely considered that diction, whether in English or not, might be inaudible – or at least, if audible, not comprehensible. Singers these days are not too interested in meaning (I should qualify this and say 'a certain type of singer'). 'Which?' I hear you ask. Well, to be brutal, I'm referring to those who see themselves as nineteenth-century singers, who cast themselves back in an abandoned manner and leap without thought into the garb of fedora hat and astrakhan collar, who consider the past world of *bel canto* and the sound of the same to be the apogee of taste and style and who, moreover, will insist on singing English with an Italian tint: 'Eet twas een Parees, O myee darleeng,' or, 'Een yourr hannd the weeponna graspeeng, eeven hee's whoa lyee therea gaspeeng.'

Generally, singers are far too lazy with their enunciation, too flaccid with their oracular equipment (at least when they sing), believing quite falsely that the percussion of words will destroy the line of the voice. This is never the truth when the voice is adequately supported, the air pressure inevitable and strong.

So what should be done? Until every man speaks all the operative languages and all singers perform with lucidity of intention and clarity of tongue, I think that an opera sung in the original language with sub-titles to aid the audience is the nearest we have to a perfect solution.

Returning to my second question, there can be no question that the opera is radically altered when performed in translation. There is no mystery here. Language is, after all, an instrument which colours as it plays. To change the instrument is to change the emotional weight of the work. *The Night Watch* of Rembrandt might be traced and painted in acrylics, but would be a very different picture. Consider, also, how a photograph of a letter is so different from the original, with its own deep scratches and sense of being intentionally and emotionally marked. Mozart wrote the clarinet quintet because he wanted it to be just that.

I have noted that, as a great maturity has landed on both audience and promoter, one facet of opera has resisted the general move towards original libretti. This is comedy. It still seems more acceptable, even in these more enlightened days, to perform a comedy in the vernacular. This is an echo of the past when the more serious issues of art were thought to be the natural habitat of the gentry, and would, especially with opera, be performed in the *argot* of the well-travelled sophisticate. Surely there can be no hint that comedy has less meaning than tragedy? This would be too stupid. Yet as one considers the history of comedy, or at least of comic scenes, it appears that it was meant for the less educated – in Shakespeare's time, the groundlings. Could it be that this tradition still informs our masters? Even at this moment I'm preparing *The Excursions of Mr Broucek* for a series of shows in Munich. The language is German. Why? The German tongue sits as ill at ease as English with this delicate and beautiful piece. Janacek's sung music is concerned only with the rhythm and cadence of Czech. Because Mr Broucek flies to the moon and then returns in time to the fifteenth century, it is thought to be funny. It is, of course, serious, as all comedy is. However, funny it is seen to be and consequently must be performed in a totally inadequate way. The principals will sing comb and paper where they should sing fiddle and dulcimer.

And so to the third point. Those singers who have found that to be employed is not a difficult task, and who count off their years in 10.30–5.30 tranches (much as do bank clerks and cabinet ministers), pay no attention to the companies who insist on vernacular performances of foreign works. They realise that the task is not worth the pecuniary reward.

There is a social division in our two major London opera houses, loosely based on the vernacular-versus-original language argument. It bears out (I think) my theory that opera and language are class-based. No, perhaps that goes too far. The difference is predominantly one not of class, but rather of temperament. Yet again it could be argued, very tentatively I admit, that the kind of temperament a person has leads him to the class he occupies.

At the one house, the first night audience considers itself established, urbane, landed (into what, we won't ask). It will take its entertainment, even listen sometimes, with the same wilful superiority that must have been evident in the courts of the Tudor and Stuart kings. (When I say must, I mean was, for Max has just confirmed it.) The public will understand bits of what it hears. Much will be lost to it unless, of course, it is of such simplicity that a well-bred slug would be at home with it and leave its trail in its warm and mindless folds. Here, a grand but dry building is used as a mirror for its audience. This blanket criticism is, of course, an exaggeration. But, as with most hyperbole, it contains a nugget of truth. At every performance, too, there are many genuine opera lovers, most of whom know more about the subject than this writer.

Down the road, you'll notice the opposite side of the same mirror. Here equally genuine lovers of music, some liberals and some Bollinger anarchists, set themselves different tasks. Equality is the mental logo here. They enquire how they might define this difficult concept. We will elevate and treasure our intellects, we will not be embarrassed by thought and deep emotion. These are major marks in the psyche of this class. Outwardly, they decide they will dress as university dons, Fabians, haversackers, William Morris clones – as useful and sensitive people dress. They will keep their building messy, slightly run down, for this is, in their eyes, in good taste, and it will be mirrored in their homes. The management will generally not employ the singers who work at the other house. They will confirm their individuality by insisting on the performance of foreign operas in the language of England. The language will isolate and fortify.

Now, surprise on surprise, how strange I find it when I notice that the boards of governors of these two places are filled with many lords, knights and other useful pieces. Why, then, should the places be so different? The division of society through temperament alone is an answer. The mountain of society is veined with an infinite number of fault lines, and within each hairline crack lurks a temperament that at first seeks to find one like its own and, having found it, wishes for its solitude again.

At one house the public endure one of the worst acoustics in Europe, and at the other seemingly sensible people applaud the mangling of masterworks by the club of an English translation. The acoustic at the other house is as near to perfection as is possible, but for my taste I find little to admire when I hear the chewing-gum English which sags over footlights and pit and which sucks colour from every note it fastens upon.

Parrot Sketch

A man wants to buy a parrot. He goes into a shop and sees three on a perch. One is a magnificent red one, one a superb blue, and the third a dowdy, dull creature with a cracked beak and its feathers dropping out.

The man says, 'I'll have the red one, please.'

The owner says, 'Well, that'll be £1000.'

'A thousand! What does it do?'

'Oh, I'm glad you asked. It sings all the parts in *Don Giovanni*.'

'In that case, I'll have the blue one.'

'Well, that one costs £3000.'

'Three thousand! What does *it* do, then?'

'It sings all the parts in the *Ring*.'

'I'll have to have the shitty one, then.'

'Don't get too excited – that one costs £10,000.'

'£10,000! Whatever does that one do, then?'

'Well, I've never heard it do anything, but the others call it Maestro.'

End

Max decided that he would die (this, he had been told, was possible). In a Faustian way (also Sophoclean – didn't the playwright say only a dead man can call himself happy?) his pact was up: he had found himself quite recently, for a minute, completely happy; this clearly was the time to go. Four hundred years was a very long time – four hundred years of singing, a close cousin of eternity. So, sitting one late evening sipping cold Horlicks through a strawberry-flavoured straw and feeling acutely aware of his mortality, he decided he *would* go, shuffle off the coil, go to the choir ineffable – no, certainly not that, that would be too much. He thought of a demented choirmaster insisting that consonants were to sound like small arms fire and that major thirds were to ring like fourths. His imagination wandered around the byways of celestial concert halls, pubs, roads. He was reminded of a joke. The leader of the LSO is sleeping in his bed. He is visited by an angel. The spirit says, 'I have good news, and bad news.'

'What are they?' says the violinist.

'The good news is that you have been chosen to lead the Heavenly Philharmonic.'

'And the bad?'

'First rehearsal ten o'clock tomorrow morning.'

As is the way with milky nightcaps, Max soon succumbed to its morphic draught. He was quickly asleep, seduced into woozy thoughts, into the dangerous, uncontrollable paths of his slippy, dark soul.

'I've spent these centuries,' he conjectured, 'singing music. Was it worth it? What have I learned?' he conjectured (again). 'Has it freed me of myself, has it given me a perspective of peace?' he ejaculated (for the first time). 'Music is art. What is art?' This second ejaculation followed *attacca staccato*.

Now, drowned in sleep, answers began to seep through the holes in Max's brain. The seepings grew, seeding their forming lines into a growing polyphony which repeated itself with only the slightest variations. The sound was similar to the glass harmonica. The music seemed to repeat itself eternally. Old, dreaming Max was reminded by the music of the vastness of identical nature and, simultaneously, the minute uniqueness of every part of it. Here was an archetypal form. He recognised it in his soul (thanks partly to his drink). He spoke to every repetition as to a new old friend. Here was a higher intelligence.

As the music reached a climax ('You see,' Max thought, 'even this is structure') a voice, a massive brass voice like that of the colossus which bestrode the harbour at Rhodes, ordered his Domestica and olives, intoned or perhaps genuinely sang in an arresting *Sprechgesang*.

Art, when shared, is a conspiracy: something which can be owned, a caramel mélange of comfort which prevents the development of the singular soul, that one, that pink tender one born with the possibility of courage and thus with understanding [*Max nearly work up, but such possible action was rendered impotent as the voice continued*] and is, in so being, light years from love.

'That's a bit of a mouthful,' conjectured and ejaculated Max (yes, both again). 'Am I to understand that all the greatest creations of man only make man feel less lonely, giving him something to cling to on his perilous path, his lethal life?'

The voice didn't answer – the effusion had weakened him. He had withdrawn *voix-de-combat*, but a final 'Domestica and olives, please' could be heard echoing down the centuries.

The voice had, however, awakened Max's holey brain. 'If this could be the truth,' he said, 'then my life has been wasted with something of little worth, with a saccharine sweetener by which reality and truth have been corrupted.'

He was, for the first time in his life, *thinking*. 'No more Horlicks for you,' his guardian angel thought.

' "Guardian angel," you said, didn't you?'

'Yes, that's right.'

'Does Max know he has one?'

'Perhaps not,' said the winged one.

'In that case, bugger off and leave Max to his ejaculations.'

Max continued: 'Wow! Cripes! Perhaps there *is* something more. Now, I am going to find out what art is without its comfort blanket.'

He thought hard, he thought *really* hard, but got nowhere. He was stumped.

Then he heard a flapping above him. He looked up and saw, wheeling and banking, an angel with rainbow wings, tipped with marine pinions, flying his way with the sound of the surfing of the wind among the lofty pines. It landed with a puff of dust and said, 'I don't see why I should be told to bugger off, especially from a character that doesn't exist.'

Calming itself (it had absolutely no genitals), it continued, 'I'll try to make your artistic past acceptable, try to make your long tired life a little more worthwhile.' It so expostulated, as angels are wont.

(At this stage, it must be admitted that Max had a narrow brain. He was no head-box, no thinker. It was sadly true that he had sometimes been bored, but usually he had lived in a general effervescent NOW which not only pleased him, but also kept his mind from deeper things – had there been any.)

Anyway, the pinions are buffeting. The angel wants to get on with it.

'Please expostulate,' Max interjected. (He could do that, too.) 'But before you tell me what art is *not*, explain to me what it can be at its best, and how perhaps I might tell good from bad.'

With a flutter (I hope it was a flutter) that caused the bedclothes to rise, the angel began: 'Max, old son, you can never begin to recognise good art from bad art if you exist in a one-dimensional intellectual plane. In this condition you cannot fly, leave yourself.' (Another major fluttering here.) 'You are imprisoned in a thinking world where everything can be proved for your own satisfaction and self-love. Yet (as you are an honest man), you have the feeling that something is missing – like egg and chips without the ketchup. The brain can create anything it desires, and from this comfortable position everything can be called art (from rice lit from behind to a house – a useful house filled with concrete). Because all of life is a miracle, this thinking is possible. Sadly, the intellect in such a welter of indiscriminate meaning feels left out. It must preen, show itself, strut its stuff (always ideas). All of this is interesting, it is true, but only to that part of us called the self, that vulnerable but inflatable nonentity. This aspect of art is mostly championed by that spiritless band called art historians, music critics, critics in general; those so full of hubris they find that to define one work they need another, a different, and should God smack them in the face they would call it a wet herring – which, of course it is. This aspect of art usually has a political programme, is concerned with issues, with the instant 'now', misinterpreting the fact of seamless, endless unity of love into a self, an ego, an I that wallows in *its* instant. The I so becomes a king, a magus, a soothsayer, a juggler of yarrows. Everything becomes a statement, an argument for the self, but at exactly the *same* time a cry of pain.'

Max stretched in his dream and said (for the second time): 'Why the pain?'

Tracey responded (isn't that crude?), 'Because a "self", of its nature, cannot bear to die, but it knows it must.'

Max, rubbing his eyes, said, 'I can see, even with my thick brain, that this also applies to music. It's true one finds the instant clever composers; then one also notices those whose music, you know, has existed forever – Stravinsky, Mozart, Birtwistle, Tippett – those who made their pieces centuries even before they were born. What is the difference, Tracey?' (for that was the angel's name – perhaps it was a girl, after all).

Tracey replied, 'Great, endless art is a mirror of love, even of rapture. It is only concerned with reflecting careless care. It has no interest in concept, self, intellect, politics. It stands free, it occupies the eternal dimension, a place from where all can be seen. Great art is not an exercise of praise or complaint. Great art puts the self completely away. Kills it.' She continued. 'You must now begin to see that as all art has been written, composed, by a *self*, then art itself, even the finest and most heavenly, *cannot* be the highest expression or the reflection of that endless light which may be called the Spirit. I would say that science, too, finds itself as distanced from eternal Love. There is little difference between art and science – people who oppose them speak only of their own temperaments, desires, needs.'

'What is art, what is science?' Max then questioned.

'Art and science – let me think. Yes, I've got it [came the thought, as if from a thought]. The first is the easy indulgence, the second the easy treadmill. In the eye of Love they are the same, simply two aspects of secular knowledge, both easy prey for those intellectual and religious rapscallions who don't know the difference between epiphany and power. The claim is that, if both are studied enough, they will eventually reveal some mystery, or tell us more of Good or Evil. There are no doubts about the Spirit, that Great Love and its total omniscience. Once you know It, are It, any other pointers to its whereabouts, whether artistic or scientific, only point towards themselves.'

With that the angel flew, scattering odd feathers as blessings. One fell on the sleeping Max and he died, ever so peacefully.

Those who wished to welcome his soul prepared his lodgings. Those who weren't aware of him continued their gossip, and those who found him 'a love', 'a nice man', wept for a while and then continued with their gossip and interesting frailties.

The void was magnificently unaware; but a sibling he was and 'it knew', in its way.

After Max's transference to other climes I lived on for some time, or I believe I did – for my voice was gone and, bereft of action, I gradually descended into that dim, eyeless world of petty thought and self-analysis. I had become enraptured with the idea that it is only by the things we make or produce that the self can be proved. My argument followed as follows.

While I consider my children, constructions, possessions, artistic debris, then I am pleasurably informed that I AM. These things have escaped from me and are a mark of ME. Then I had two thoughts. The first was that I didn't recognise any of the things that I had created – they must have been a part of me, but were not party of my instant passing now. They could all have been made by anyone else. The personal touch was another's. I did recognise them in a certain cold way, but they were obviously free things that owed me nothing.

My second thought led me to consider that, as all these strange things were of my making, my understanding, what part did they play in the evaluation of myself? Were they, in fact, a substitute for me? Were they preventing knowledge of the self? The answer to these questions was Yes. In that case, I thought, I must look, really look at me. What did I find?

I discovered a strange shell – recognisable, it is true, in its infirmity, but certainly not understood. This shell surrounded a vacuum; a true emptiness, a terrifying hole. I was aware of no head, eyes, vitals, only the clang of a door and the dark of a cell. I believed that I had proved my own point, and sat in masochistic pleasure when a small chink appeared under a rib, a shaft of warm light showed through and an idea in red appeared. Soon, all of the emptiness was filled. The idea nurtured, loved, and then it left. I was empty again. The same action then occurred again and again. I found that I was not separate from what I made, for my essence was in the constancy of making. There was no stopping it, no holding.

But there would be a stop, and I vaguely remember, too, sitting – or was it lying? – in a pleasant but unknown room, looking at and truly considering an old hand as if it was a new masterpiece, and throwing off my clothes with the pure carelessness of a baby, and of seeing a timeless light.

I realised, quite late, that Max and myself were one. He was the singer with the guts that I was frightened to be. I was the arrogant commentator, hiding, never quite to be seen in the light. Between us we made it, but it was touch and go.

AMO ERGO SUM